Dynamic Adventure

A Guide to Starting and Shaping Missional Churches

Dynamic Adventure

A Guide to Starting and Shaping Missional Churches

DANIEL STEIGERWALD
DEBORAH LOYD
APRIL TE GROOTENHUIS CRULL
& MICHAEL KUDER

COMMUNITAS
— International —

www.gocommunitas.org

Christian Associates International, Inc.
dba
Communitas International
2221 E. Arapahoe Rd #3338
Centennial, CO 80161
www.gocommunitas.org
E-mail: usoffice@gocommunitas.org

Cover and Graphics: Robin Renard | www.edustries.com
Design and Layout: Jeremie Malengreaux | www.edustries.com

www.thedynamicadventure.com

TABLE OF CONTENTS

WELCOME

A *Dynamic Adventure* is best experienced with others! Our hope is that you will walk through this workbook together with a local group of dreamers, practitioners, or church planters excited to make a difference in your city with the good news of Jesus. We invite you to participate in the worldwide community forming at www.thedynamicadventure.com where you'll find a growing collection of additional material, training, videos, and coaching. At thedynamicadventure.com you'll find a great place to connect with other adventurers to share stories and best practices from your very own *Dynamic Adventure!*

PREFACE

We believe you are reading this book because you are passionate about spreading the good news of God's Kingdom. This yearning consumes us too. We in Communitas long to see more culture-sensitive churches sowing the gospel so that as many people as possible might experience the love of Jesus. This compels us to do our best to listen to practitioners who are engaging local contexts and trying to create new forms of church. What are they discovering? What is stirring their hearts? For years we've been paying attention to what they're saying. This is what we're hearing repeated time and time again across the world:

> We want to see new forms of church emerge that bring the many people we know and love into life-giving engagement with Jesus. These friends don't know Christ, or if they do, they have little to do with church. We can't imagine them ever becoming part of any church we know. And yet we realize we cannot leave the church out of the picture just because we don't see how our friends could fit in.
>
> We don't want more churches that convert people to a religious culture that separates them from the world. Instead, we dream of churches that engage culture and support the good found there,

but who also show healthier ways to live where culture entraps people in damaging or unjust practices.

> We desire an authentic journey with Jesus and with others who love Christ. We don't want to be "posers." We want to invite others into a way of life that we ourselves are finding transformative – a life that is satisfying and real, that helps us rest in Jesus' love while loving others the way Christ did.
>
> We feel deep down that there must be new, less conventional ways to be the body of Christ. And yet we also desire to do our part to mature any form of church to be all that God intends her to be. We want to see a greater variety of context-sensitive churches that stand for Jesus, point to Christ's Kingdom, and provide a foretaste in the here and now of God's Kingdom that is coming.

Although we commonly hear such themes repeated, we also hear people say:

> We know we cannot journey alone as a single, isolated faith community. We know we need to join hands and hearts with the broader body of Christ.
>
> We're not trying to create a Christian utopia, but

we know much more is possible than what we now see. We want to live into the prayer Jesus gives us, imploring God to, "Let Your Kingdom come; Let Your will be done, on earth, as it is in heaven." And we, both women and men alike, believe our efforts are meant to be a part of God's answer to that very prayer.

Does any of this resonate with you? Is your heart also stirred in such ways? We in Communitas sense a calling to establish churches that follow Jesus in transforming their world. If you can relate to the longings expressed here, we invite you to gather some other dreamers and dig into the ideas and activities in this book. We have written it with the hope that it might help you and others experiment together to develop fresh expressions of church. Perhaps the ache you also feel is nothing less than the nudging of the Spirit of God? If so, please dig in...and prepare yourself for a dynamic adventure!

INTRODUCTION

What you hold in your hands is not a manual full of lessons on how to effectively start and shape a church. Instead, it's a guidebook for an adventure that by nature will not conform itself to any technique or defined pathway to success. Missional church planting is an ever changing, wild, and unpredictable experience, much like the adventure of exploring a thriving city for the first time. A city has a life of its own, the complex product of countless interactions between millions of people on a daily basis. And the landscape can change quickly too. A desolate street can transform overnight into a thriving marketplace. The patrons in a café differ from hour to hour. Art exhibits change regularly. Missional church planting can be like that too, as people and circumstances often change quickly.

This guidebook is a tool designed to equip you as an explorer. To get the most out of visiting a historic city like Amsterdam, for instance, you might pick up a guidebook to read before you get there, to gain back-ground information and know what to expect in your travels. Later you take it with you to make sense out of the sights, historic places, and cultural challenges.

A good city-guide deepens your understanding and appreciation of what you are experiencing. But it doesn't merely show you the sights; it teaches you the skills you need to thrive in the city. It won't simply tell you where to eat; it will explain to you the city's food culture and how to find a great restaurant on your own. A good city-guide will not only tell you to walk to a specific metro stop, but it will also teach you how to navigate the nuances of the mass transit system.

That's the intention behind this guidebook. As missional church planters, many of us are beginning a journey into strange and unfamiliar territory. We want to give you the tools you need to thrive on the adventure. Toward that end we hope that you will take this guidebook with you on your journey as you explore, imagine, and discover what church could look like for the people you're meeting in your local context! And if your team has already journeyed for years and established a presence in your city as a local church, we also hope you will see this guidebook as an invaluable aid to help you more deeply engage your surroundings, mature as a faith community, and deepen your Kingdom impact.

To get the most out of this adventure, we recommend

you use this book in a specific way. The introductory material below instructs you on how to do that, so we encourage you not to simply skim across the surface but take time to grasp what we're saying. When we explore a new city, our experience is often richer when we've studied books, websites, and travel shows prior to our arrival. In like manner, we believe your team's church planting journey will be greatly enriched by taking the time to interact with the background material we've included below.

How to use this guide

1. **Walk through this guidebook with your team.**
   Whatever the makeup of your team - whether you're a loosely affiliated group of dreamers hoping to impact your city, a small band of pioneers intending to plant a church, or the leadership core of an established church - we strongly encourage you to walk through this guidebook together. We've specifically designed it to provoke group processing, interaction, and team building.

2. **Leverage the exercises.** We've designed learning exercises throughout the book to help you progress from gaining essential background knowledge to practically applying and evaluating what you have learned. They incorporate your own thoughts, feelings, and actions to deepen learning and provide transformational experiences. In this guidebook, you will learn new information, relate it to your own experience, and then act on that learning.

   The learning exercises will be accomplished in various modes or stages: individual work, work with a mentor, partner work, small group work, and finally, through work with your team. The typical flow will go from individual or small group explorations and then flow outward to the larger team.

Symbols for Learning Exercises:

 Personal learning exercise

 Mentor learning exercise

 Partner learning exercise

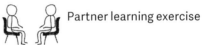 Small group learning exercise

 Team learning exercise

We recognize that team sizes vary. If your team is larger than four people, when the exercises instruct you to work in small groups, break up into groups of four or less. If your team is fewer than four people, do all "small group" activities as a team. Groups need to be smaller than four so everyone gives input. Research shows that size and physical space matter for small group learning. We recommend you sit in circles for small group work.

You will find a list of supplies that you will need to have on hand at the beginning of each learning exercise. We've also included a rough estimate of the time required to complete each exercise. It is, however, only an estimate. Your time will vary depending on a variety of factors such as the number of people on your team and how deeply you engage the exercise.

For each learning exercise you will need a facilitator. This person will take responsibility for creating an atmosphere that is conducive to the learning goals by:

- Ensuring that everyone is respected.
- Allowing everyone to talk and "be heard" by the group.
- Affirming what is said; there are no correct answers to learning exercises.

3. **Start with your unique experience.** After reading the brief introduction in the next chapter, determine where the bulk of your work as a group, team, or church is needed. Plan to spend a significant amount of time digging into and working with the contents in that chapter.

However, because all of the dynamics you'll be exploring are present at each point in a church plant, also plan to work through the other chapters. Pick and choose exercises as they seem relevant to your group.

4. **Complete the Missional Action Plan.** Each chapter concludes with a special debriefing exercise – MAP It! – to guide your team to turn your learning into actionable plans. Follow the instructions to develop your team's Missional Action Plan at the end of the book. This tool is meant to be flexible and to serve you and your team. We recognize that every team is at a different stage of development, so the dynamic that best describes where you are will likely have the most action points. But each dynamic can also have one that is appropriate for your current experience. Try to make these action points as concrete as possible, including deadlines and areas of accountability.

5. **Journal your experience.** At the end of each chapter we've included a few blank pages intended as a space for you to reflect on what you've learned in the chapter. Write down whatever is important to you: notes on key concepts, areas to investigate further, actions you need to take, etc.

6. **Find a coach/mentor.** An experienced coach can be an invaluable asset to you and your team as you work through this material. Communitas provides coaching to all of its project teams, as do other church planting organizations. Consult with your network or denomination and see what help is available. Or reach out to Communitas - we'd love to talk with you. Coaching and mentoring is often available in person or online.

A Common Starting Point

Before we set out on our adventure, we want to be sure that we have a common starting point. We all bring our own understanding of language and culture to the table. We believe it's important that we clarify our language and share our background assumptions so that you can get the most benefit from this workbook.

Some Important Definitions

In this guidebook we use certain words that have different meanings in different contexts. We want to be clear from the beginning what we mean by these words:

Missionary: We use the word *missionary*. This is not a popular word in many cultures, and for good reason. At times the Church has united with the State to send missionaries who have delivered a confusing mix of religion, Jesus, and Western culture. At its worst this has led to exploiting foreign peoples rather than finding God at work within them. We go back to the original meaning of the word: "a sent one." Not ones sent to a distant land or to a far off people, but simply ones sent from God, in Jesus's name, to announce God's good news, both in word and deed. When using this guidebook, leave room for the word missionary to carry a positive meaning; think like the Apostle Paul, who echoed the ancient phrase, "How beautiful are the feet of those who bring good news." [1]

Team: Throughout the guidebook we will be referring to a *team*. As we noted above, this might be a small group, an elder board, a church planting team, or a group of people with a similar hope. You can choose to define *team* however you want, but we assume you are working through this book with others who have similar hopes and dreams.

Leadership: Author Ken Blanchard defines leadership as the capacity to influence people. [2] We cover this subject in greater depth in chapter six; however, we want to clearly state up front that we believe everyone can exert influence in some way. Leading is not an elite function. Good leadership actually gives permission to each person to bring healthy voice and influence to the team. In this book, when we mention leadership, we are talking about people who are exerting influence and making decisions. [3]

Missional Initiative: This is a team-based effort in a city that intentionally seeds the ground to grow communities that could become new churches or expressions of church. In Communitas we believe that missional initiatives and similar projects perform a vital role in preparing the ground for church planting.

---

1   Romans 10:15.

2   Ken Blanchard, *Leading at a Higher Level* (Upper Saddle River: FT Press, 2010), xvi.

3   As Communitas enters a given city for church planting, we don't insist that a "team leader" come onto the scene to get things started; rather, we encourage missionary teams to engage their context and start learning as much as they can about their local environment. An appropriately gifted team leader will most often be required as a missional initiative gains momentum. However, Communitas believes the expression of Christ's Kingdom on earth is not dependent on superstars. We applaud any step of faith a team takes to set the stage for the emergence of local churches - you never know what Jesus will do through faithful men and women engaging their context!

Church: We can hardly talk about church planting without also creating room for understanding how we're defining the word. We're going to take a bit more space to unpack what we mean by this, since the mission of Communitas is to follow Jesus in establishing these local bodies we call churches.

So what is "church" at its most basic level? A.W. Tozer began his book *The Knowledge of the Holy* with the words, "What comes into our minds when we think about God is the most important thing about us." By those words he meant that our unique experiences, circumstances, and information combine to form our perception of The Almighty. It's the same way with our definitions of church. What we have individually experienced, learned from Bible study, what our culture has shaped us to think, and many more factors unique to each of us - all converge to form in us a perception of what church ought to be.

In many cases the word *church* brings to mind a site or place where regular worship services, classes, and spiritual events are conducted. Our minds also go to various words like simple, multi-site, house church, mega-church, contemporary, liturgical, seeker-sensitive - and yes, even missional - among many others. We believe that God uses many different forms of church as well as many different approaches to church to achieve His purposes in the world. But neither *form* nor *approach* are what we want to focus on in our definition of church.

Instead, we'd like to zoom in on the elemental *functions* we believe comprise church. We believe that at its core, an expression of church exists when three basic functions are present: communion, community, and mission. Get a group of people experiencing God,

engaging in redemptive community, and partnering with Jesus in His kingdom work, and that is an expression of church. The beauty of this framework is that it encompasses every kind of church, from the organic home-based group in Madrid, Spain impacting the artist community, to the 2,000 member international church with three big services in Amsterdam, the Netherlands. It fits the community in St. Paul, USA, who by serving the neediest of their city, are bringing people into Christ-centered communion and community, just as it fits a group in Sao Paulo, Brazil, gathering around Bible teaching videos, sharing life, and serving together.

We have found that staying focused on the *functions* of communion, community, and mission and allowing *form* to develop organically from context is incredibly freeing to church planters around the world. Teams can focus on practicing the elements of communion, community, and mission, and these activities set the stage for expressions of church to be birthed. Of course, like every living thing, churches have life stages. From conception to birth, infancy to adolescence and beyond, churches grow and change, too.

Nonetheless, our belief is that community, communion, and mission ought to be at the core of any healthy church, regardless of life stage. What will likely change is how these functions are expressed at any given stage, not whether they are present. In chapters four and five ahead, we'll take a closer look at how teams and churches might express these three vital functions in ways that uniquely suit them. For now, let's take a moment and consider what "church" means not only to Communitas, but also to you.

What is Church?

Time: 60 to 90 minutes
Supplies: Blank paper, pencils or pens, whiteboard and markers, sticky-notes

Our definition of church greatly impacts our methods and goals for church planting. This exercise is designed to help you think through communion, community, and mission as the basic functions of church.

1. Each person folds a blank sheet of paper into three columns. Label the columns "communion," "community," and "mission." Take five minutes alone to write down in the respective column words, phrases, or actions that you associate with each function.

2. After five minutes, gather in small groups of four or less to discuss what you came up with for communion, community, and mission. How does framing church within these functions help you understand what church could be? If it is not helpful, what functions would you add?

3. Reviewing each person's contribution for communion, community, and mission, small groups write on sticky-notes their top three words, phrases, or actions that best describe how they define church. Write one concept per sticky-note.

4. Come together as a team. Groups take turns posting their notes on the whiteboard and sharing their concepts.

5. The facilitator assists the team in grouping and evaluating the most important concepts to create a definition of church. The team assesses and amends the definition until they are satisfied with it. The facilitator writes the final definition on the whiteboard.

Our Background Assumptions

Below are the assumptions we bring to this guide. We encourage teams to interact over them, or certain parts of the chapters ahead may be confusing. The degree to which we hold these assumptions in common can enhance our ability to function as a team, so this is no trivial matter.

- God is a God of mission. We understand this from the Bible, which we take to be divinely inspired, fully and authoritatively reliable as the Storyline from which we get our bearings. We do our best

to stay true to this Story, and obedient, by the power of God's Spirit, to all that God in Christ asks of us in this living Word.

- In Christ's coming as a human being, God gives us a flesh and blood lesson on who God is. In Jesus, we see God's forgiveness and unfailing love toward all people. And we also see God's intention to renew all things, to bring heaven down to earth and establish a new order where the knowledge of the Lord fills the earth. God the Father and Jesus the Son commission God's people, the Church, to go into the world in the power of the Spirit to demonstrate and proclaim God's reign over all creation. With Jesus as the Head, the body of Christ in all its local expressions is meant to be a living, tangible expression of God's presence and loving intention for all humanity. Local churches exist so that people everywhere might choose to put their hope in Jesus Christ and grow as His disciples.

- To be "missional" means we are doing our best to follow Christ into God's mission for the sake of the world. To be a "missional community" in our local setting means we commit ourselves as a group to intentionally make more and better disciples who are equipped as missionaries to live and proclaim God's kingdom. In doing this, we work with the Spirit to "incarnate" (embody) Jesus' presence and love in the world.

- Communitas' mission is *to establish churches who follow Jesus in transforming their world."* Our core values are described by these three phrases: Kingdom-seeking, grace-oriented, and people-focused. As a result of our mission and our values, we are highly motivated to train people for sustainable mission and church planting.

- We believe that success in mission and church planting is measured, first and foremost, by faithfulness. A team moving forward and following Jesus as best they can will never be cast as a failure, even if the project does not take root. We believe it takes the sowing of many seeds, along with a lot of cooperative watering of those seeds, to see incarnational churches birthed and multiplied. As the Apostle Paul reminds us, "the Lord has assigned to each his task...neither the one who plants nor the one who waters is anything, but only God, who makes things grow. The one who plants and the one who waters have one purpose, and they will each be rewarded according to their own labor. For we are co-workers in God's service..."[4]

- Last but not least, we realize that those who use this guide come from many different backgrounds and cultures, language groups, and theological perspectives. We would, therefore, expect that the content would be applied differently from one context to another. This guide itself is meant to be flexible and adaptable, not applied rigidly.

Most missionary and church planting teams start their journey together with great excitement. But too often, after a short time they discover that some team members have had their own hidden expectations, that is, their own unspoken assumptions about what the team should believe and do. Assumptions are not evil; as a matter of fact, we all have them. However, if certain assumptions are held in secret, they can become a divisive force within teams. Hidden assumptions can even lead to people leaving a team unnecessarily. So we encourage teams from the start to bring their assumptions to the table, just as we have sought to do so above.

The following learning exercise is designed to help you compare and contrast your assumptions about mission with those that Communitas holds. However, you as a team will also, with a few adjustments, be able to use this format with your teammates to spark conversation over differences in core assumptions. This will help you build bridges of understanding, thus creating a stronger team over time.

---

4   I Cor. 3:7-9.

Interacting with Communitas' Background Assumptions

Time: 30 to 45 minutes
Supplies: Blank sheet of paper, pen or pencil

1. Individuals fold a blank sheet of paper in half lengthwise. Think of what your assumptions about God, mission, and church might be, and then on the left hand side write five or six of them.

2. Now re-read Communitas' assumptions described above, and underline the key phrases in each statement.

3. On the right side of the paper write the phrases that you underlined. Draw lines to connect those on the right that correspond with those on the left. Circle the statements on either side that do not have a corresponding assumption.

4. With a partner, compare and contrast your assumptions with those of Communitas. Then process your partner's list. Discuss what needs to happen to bring each list into reasonable agreement with Communitas' assumptions. Where do you differ? Are these fatal differences, are they "agree to disagree," or can they be reconciled? Write in your notes and changes.

Dynamics for a "Dynamic Adventure"

We've looked briefly at how to use this guidebook, and we've given you some key definitions and background assumptions to help give us a common starting point for what's ahead. Now we'd like to briefly introduce Communitas' approach to missional church planting. We ourselves are still on a journey of discovery, but through our interaction with missionaries in diverse nations over many years, we have begun to observe a consistent pattern of core behaviors present in teams trying to start, shape, and multiply missional churches. We are continually striving to better understand and *describe* that pattern of behaviors, especially as we see them exhibited by our missional initiatives, church plants, and established churches. There is always more to learn! But let it be clear from the start: we are not trying to *prescribe* a technique or particular model of church planting we want teams to imitate. There is an important distinction between the words *describe* and *prescribe*!

When we describe a pattern, we are not saying, "Follow these steps and you will succeed in planting a context-sensitive church." We don't believe there is a formula or step-by-step plan to success for the kind of church planting we are talking about, or we would indeed prescribe it! What we are saying is, "Here's a group of six behaviors that we commonly find active in sustainable, reproducing expressions of church that draw people to Jesus and equip them to think, act, and live like Him." We have chosen to call these behaviors *dynamics* because that word captures the idea of ongoing motion or action.[5]

You will see below that we actually use six verbs to describe each of the dynamics – again, because we see them as continuous motions. The adventure of missional church planting is never static but ever active. That's why we find it appropriate to entitle this book, "Dynamic Adventure!" We envision church planting teams (and even leaders of established churches) keeping these behaviors active throughout their entire lives. This guide will help your team activate each of the dynamics over time, with your own discerned timeline and way of operating in view. When teams give attention to cultivating each of these over the long haul, we have observed them growing in health and impact. Our hope is that that will be your experience, too.

Notice above that we do not say anything about growth in numbers, nor do we mention anything about some ideal model we have in view. Like a good city-guide, these dynamics are not about defining THE WAY forward, as if they map out the perfect route to engaging your city and getting you to a desired destination. Instead, they equip you to engage your context as your adventure unfolds before you.

The dynamics we mention below are the repetitive

motions all travelers will likely engage in. The dynamics provide a framework for all of our interaction ahead, so we encourage your team to spend some time together wrestling with their meaning and relevance. We close this chapter with an exercise to help you begin that wrestling. In the next chapters we'll explore each dynamic in greater detail and show their practical value, to help you apply them to your unique situation.

Communitas' "dynamic" approach to missional church planting involves continuous attention to these behaviors:

Embed = *root in context and relational networks as an enriching presence*
Initiate = *establish a coordinated gospel-sowing response across an area and/or group*
Practice = *express the identity and Jesus life you're inviting others into*
Mature = *develop as a unique, local expression of the body of Christ*
Hub = *cultivate local environments to multiply missional initiatives and churches*
Extend = *help fuel trans-local movements for church planting beyond the city*

The following exercise is meant to engage your imagination around the six dynamics. It's a time simply for creative brainstorming. You are not asked to act on any idea at this point but to let your imagination run away with you. Later on we will introduce a learning exercise that will invite you to come up with concrete actionable items. For now just imagine as if you had no restraints.

---

5   Meriam Webster's online dictionary defines "dynamic" as: "marked by usually continuous and productive activity or change." See http://www.merriam-webster.com/dictionary/dynamic.

Stirring Your Imagination for Communitas' Church Planting Approach

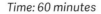

Time: 60 minutes
Supplies: Blank paper and pencil or pen

1. In small groups of four or less review the verbs and the one-line descriptions for each of the six dynamics above. Go around the circle taking turns reading each one aloud. A note-taker lists each dynamic on a sheet of paper equally spaced so that there is room below each one.

2. As you study these verbs and descriptors, what comes to mind? Group members suggest anything that comes to mind and the note-taker records it. This can be an action, an emotion, a descriptive word, a sensory experience, or a symbol. What do these words, actions, emotions, or sensory experiences prompt you to do? What actions could you take to enact the six dynamics for church planting?

3. Take turns describing to your small group what you dream about for church planting. Remember this does not have to be practical. It is an exercise in dreaming. Hold each other's dreams reverently!

4. Gather together as a team. When prompted, each small group shares their dream with the larger team. Flesh out your dream as much as possible. The team is invited to ask questions or give comments.

What's Our Next Step?

In the Preface and in this Introduction we've explored with you why we've developed this guidebook, and how your team can use it. We have also invited you to process some key definitions and assumptions, including how Communitas at the most basic level describes the six dynamics we commonly find activated among teams that succeed in planting incarnational churches. In the opening chapter ahead, we'll dig into stories and deeper descriptions of the six dynamics. We'll also explore the inner terrain of how we see ourselves, and how our identity relates to how and why we do mission.

 MAP It!

Here's your first chance to try out the Missional Action Plan. Turn to Appendix A in the back of the book to begin your MAP. Take a few minutes to read the introduction and instructions. Then, in the section under *Vision* write out your team's preliminary thoughts on the hopes, dreams, and values of your project or church. Next, skip down to the *Basics of Church* section. Write in any thoughts your team may have about communion, community, and mission. Don't worry, there's no test, and we'll come back to this section later. It's just good to get your initial ideas on paper.

My Reflections:

What questions do you have about Communitas?

What are your hopes for your experience with this guide?

What worked for you?

What do you need more of?

What was your takeaway?

PART ONE - THE BASICS: PACKING FOR THE JOURNEY AHEAD

Wow! We've already started putting you to work, and that was just the Introduction! In this opening part of the guide, we are devoting attention to building a good foundation. We want you and your team to move forward armed with a good grasp of the meaning and relevance of the six church planting dynamics. We also want to dig down and tap into the fountain of our motivation and passion, which relates to how we see ourselves – our identity. In Communitas, we believe ministry flows out of being, out of an inner sense of calling. We encourage you not to rush through these two opening chapters, since they will enable you to get much more out of the rest of this book.

Chapter 1 – Exploring a Dynamic Approach

So far, we have given you a very brief introduction to the six church planting dynamics. In this chapter we'll help you discover their fuller meaning and how each of the dynamics relates to the work of your team. Finally, we'll help you explore how the six dynamics together form a unique approach to missional church planting. As you go through the guidebook, you will find more stories, explanations, and exercises to help you understand and apply each specific dynamic. So don't worry if you don't quite understand it all yet.

Discovering the Six Dynamics

Moving beyond a simple verb and one-liner description of each dynamic, the following paragraphs summarize the six dynamics. When operative, each makes its own unique contribution to forming expressions of church that positively impact the people and places they engage. Take some time to read each one, underlining key words or phrases that aid your understanding.

Embed = *root in context and relational networks as an enriching presence*

Embedding happens when all members of a team engage in a missionary lifestyle. They reach beyond their cultural subset into the complex diversity common to any city. They work to become cultural insiders by absorbing as much knowledge as they can about their context, while also relating to local people and serving alongside them where possible. As a church matures, it is vital for it to continue to *embed* well. The church must continue to root in context and cultivate relationships as an enriching presence. Without an intentional outward focus, churches invariably turn their focus and energy inward toward themselves.

Initiate = *establish a coordinated gospel-sowing response across an area and/or group*

Initiating is discerning or deciding what to do with all the insider knowledge of local culture, the new relationships, and the many service opportunities discovered through a team's missionary activity. Discernment enables the team to focus its gospel-sowing activities so that it is engaging its context in ways that are life-giving and sustainable. The team is more focused and intentional in both their individual and community evangelism efforts. Initiating does not mean the team steps back from *embedding*, but it chooses to be more strategic in directing its

missionary activities so that an inclusive and sustainable missional community might be formed. Over time, as the community gains momentum and people, it will have the capacity to expand its spheres of gospel-sowing.

Practice = *express the identity and Jesus life you're inviting others into*

Practicing occurs as teams begin to live into a common group identity (vision, values, name, theology, etc.). It also involves experimenting with or testing a discipleship rhythm together to see what practices help the team grow, spiritually and communally, as they engage their context. By expressing an identity and discipleship rhythm the missionary team is able to credibly invite people into a communal identity and way of life that they themselves have found transformative. Rallying around an identity and way of life also protects the forming community from the whims of newcomers who often come in with a desire to create their own version of church. Identity and spiritual practices are not static or immovable, but over long periods of time will change as the community grows and responds both to its members and also to its host culture.

Mature = *develop as a unique, local expression of the body of Christ*

Maturing happens as a faith community intentionally develops into a more sustainable form, giving appropriate attention to systems and processes that support its growth and health. The community shows a clear public face (unless that is deemed unwise due to contextual factors), and generally becomes more visible and accessible to the host context as an identifiable local entity or "church."[6] As a body it stands on its own two feet, no longer dependent on the original planting team. While remaining attentive to vision, the church becomes seasoned in its capacity to govern itself, to apprentice people in the way of Jesus, to release the giftedness of the body, and to sustain itself financially. This *maturing* enables the body to vividly display the gospel and goodness of God, so that it both points to and gives people tastes of the coming Kingdom of God.

Hub = *cultivate local environments to multiply missional initiatives and churches*

Hubbing involves creating or participating in environments locally that foster the multiplication of new missional initiatives and church plants. It happens more significantly as the church gains enough momentum to invest in key partnerships for church planting across the city. However, pioneering teams can also activate this dynamic early on if they can intentionally harness the energy, gifts, and resources needed to both mature their own project and also incubate new church planting initiatives. Whether it's in the early startup years or later on,

the planting team or church *hubs* by drawing upon its own resources and those of other like-minded missional networks for the clear purpose of training and releasing teams to start new missional initiatives and churches.

Extend = *help fuel trans-local movements for church planting beyond the city*

Extending is closely related to *hubbing* but involves intentionally developing wider connections and networks that reach beyond a church's host city. Leadership teams collaborate and share resources across cities, nations, and continents to seed new missional initiatives and church expressions. As with local *hubbing*, the timing and extent of a team or church's participation in multiplying new missional initiatives and churches beyond its city will depend on its internal capacities, resources, and vision for church multiplication.

The Six Dynamics in Action

To help you grasp the meaning of the primary actions commonly at work in missional church planting, we have organized them into six distinct dynamics. However, in real time church planting involves a dance of all these – a dance that is messy at times and that looks very different from project to project. A team would ideally cultivate all these dynamics over the long haul. But a team might spend more time with certain ones, depending on their unique vision, discernment, stage of development, and spectrum of giftedness. Consider the way a group of related churches in Spain has experienced the six dynamics so far. Troy Cady, founding pastor of Oasis Madrid, gives us a brief look into that unfolding story:

---

6   We want to make room for non-conventional expressions of church that may not become identifiable local churches. Because most church planting will involve the emergence of longer-term, local bodies of Christ with the characteristics of the local churches described by the New Testament writers, from this point onward we generally use the word "church" to describe specific local churches. While opting for this usage, if your team is starting an expression of church that effectively disciples people and yet would not fit the category of "a local church," we encourage you to apply the six dynamics in light of your unique expression. Don't be hindered by our word choice - the dynamics and most of the exercises should still apply to you!

Prior to moving to Madrid, Spain in early 2002, two Communitas families (the Cadys and Wallaces) conducted some research. We wanted to know where it would be best for us to live since we had in mind to plant a church that would serve the international community. We discovered a pocket in the northwest corridor, supported by a few international schools. Since our goal was to live near English-speaking internationals and have plenty of opportunity to build friendships, that is where we decided to live.

During our first six months, we simply met people, shared meals, and held parties. If we happened to meet folks who were already Christian, we'd share with them our desire to start a church in which unchurched folks would feel at home. That fall, we banded together with a group of people we had met to begin going through the Alpha Course. We organized it in three different small groups that met in different locations on different days.

From there, we knew the groups would want to start meeting together as a large group regularly, so we began meeting weekly to take a look at our core values, purposes, and vision. We coupled this with worship so as to begin cultivating some foundational discipleship practices. By the end of that period, we had a decision to make about "going public" with the project we called Mountainview. Would we begin holding regular weekly church services?

We decided to try holding monthly large-group services while emphasizing the multiplication of small groups that met on a weekly basis. Our small groups sought to fulfill all four of our major purposes—which included worship, fellowship, discipleship, and outreach. This strategy was coupled with a few streams designed to develop leaders (such as a monthly leaders' gathering and a training manual) so the church could continue to multiply ministries.

Over the course of three "seasons" of ministry (autumn through spring,) the church's small groups multiplied from 3 (in the fall of 2002) to 13 (in the spring of 2005). During the course of this multiplication, Mountainview developed along

two geographic pockets: one pocket was in the northwest suburbs and the other was in the city. After trying for at least a year to coalesce the two pockets into one church, eventually we decided to make the city cluster distinct from the suburb cluster. Thus was born Oasis.

Both clusters then took the opportunity to take a fresh look at their core practices and rhythms for discipleship, worship, and outreach. Mountainview saw it needed to move to weekly large group services and Oasis re-imagined their way of being church.

Oasis began holding large group events every week that were varied in their purposes. Sometimes a corporate worship service was held while other times the corporate gathering was intended to bolster outreach or fellowship. Meanwhile, Oasis put in place an intentional process for making disciples that juxtaposed a season of mentoring with one-time celebrations that involved the larger body.

All the while, both churches continued to empower teams of people for fresh expressions of outreach. Both Mountainview and Oasis found ways of serving the needs of those in financial need, and eventually they collaborated together to host Madrid's first Serve the City project in 2007.

Oasis had an internship program to disciple young leaders in mission. Many of those who participated in the program over the years went on to be staff with Communitas.

As Oasis grew, a group of people emerged who had it on their hearts to establish a work for Spaniards and other Spanish-speaking people. In particular, a neighborhood right in the heart of the city (named Malasaña) served as the touchstone. Oasis commissioned a team to begin a work there in the fall of 2009.

The Malasaña group (led by the Crulls) began by taking a deep look at the neighborhood and what the needs were. The group prayed and worshipped together. They dug into the Scriptures together and supported one another spiritually. They dreamed together. They discerned a tangible project to bless the neighborhood and hosted developing leaders so as to ignite their missional imagination, sending them out. Decoupage is now a church led by and reaching Spanish people in this neighborhood.

But the Malasaña project is not the end of the story. In 2013, a team of people came together to begin dreaming about another church plant in Valencia, Spain (on the east coast, about 4 hours away from Madrid). Amy Swacina and Jonathan Steele co-lead the project, both of whom are part of the Oasis extended family. Additionally, new Spanish church planters are being trained in all three Madrid churches.

This is just the beginning. It will be exciting to see how the story continues to unfold. God's Spirit never ceases to amaze!

Let's pray that these four projects, and other initiatives that are already under way, will know how to work together in a spirit of cooperation with one another and with other churches to clearly reflect and proclaim God's glory and goodness across Spain.

Over time groups of people who are passionate about the same things tend to develop their own in-house language. This language or "shop talk" can be confusing to outsiders and to those who are new to the group. We want to help everyone understand the dynamics of church planting and to be able to pass that meaning on to others. This exercise will help us get on the same page for the dynamics we'll be investing so much energy into.

Illustrating the Dynamics of Missional Planting

Time: 90 to 120 minutes (60 to do steps 1-4, and 30 to 60 to do step 5)
Supplies: Cardstock, glue, magazines, pens or pencils, highlighters, and markers

1. As you consider Troy's account above on the development of Mountainview, Oasis, Decoupage, and Valencia, go back and identify where you think the dynamics are represented. Using a different colored marker or symbol for each dynamic, draw a circle around or highlight the parts of that story that seem to relate to the six dynamics and note which dynamic applies.

2. Now look again at the brief descriptions of each dynamic. Underline any words or concepts that are confusing to you or that you think might be confusing to others in your context.

3. With your mentor's guidance, jot down a short definition for each confusing word or concept and suggest one or two alternate words that could be used.

4. Once you are comfortable with word and concept meanings, find images in magazines (or sketch your own) that represent *Embed, Initiate, Practice, Mature, Hub,* and *Extend.* Glue them to a piece of card-stock paper. Be creative!

5. Explain each image and its corresponding concept to your mentor.

In the early stages of establishing sustainable local churches, the above dynamics generally unfold as a *progression* of activities. This word captures the idea of a natural sequence without suggesting a strictly linear, step-by-step process. Imagine a stone thrown into a still pond where the initial impact creates a ripple that expands outward in all directions, and we're perhaps closer to what we have in mind. As a team plunges into context, the impact of their Kingdom work will gradually spread out and become more apparent over time. In other words, a missionary team hoping to establish a church will start by *embedding* in context. Over time this will lead to *initiating* a strategic response to context, and as the team begins to cohere and gain momentum, *practicing* an identity and discipleship rhythm will become prominent. As growth and complexity increases, the forming community will spend more energy with activities related to *maturing* into a visible, local body ("a" church). With its internal development strengthened, the church will naturally participate in *hubbing* to incubate new church plants, and over time to even *extend* this Kingdom participation well beyond their city.

Any initial sequence in these six dynamics, however, quickly gives way to an overlapping pattern of activities. The initial ripple expands outward, but each previous dynamic remains active and is blended into the next dynamic until we have a pulsating group, where all dynamics are tended to as part of the stewardship of church planting movement(s). In the life cycle of a project, Communitas would expect to see these six dynamics interwoven and operating to varying degrees at the same time, depending on the unique situation and developmental cycle of that project or church.

A maturing church may take years to have the energy and resources to develop meaningful *hubbing* and *extending* activities. Many projects may spend the bulk of their energies tending to the first four dynamics, without much attention given at all to creating *hubbing* and *extending* activities. Communitas encourages every project to participate on some level in local and trans-local networks that focus on multiplying missional initiatives and churches. However, that participation must be appropriate to each unique project; teams are not expected to implement *hubbing* and *extending* activities beyond their capacity to do so.

One last issue regarding this pattern for missional church planting is how the dynamics interrelate. In Communitas we see the six dynamics forming three natural pairings that work in tandem to achieve distinct purposes. *Embed* and *initiate* work in tandem to *infuse missional DNA. Practice* and *mature* involve interrelated activities that *shape healthy expressions of church*. And *hub* and *extend* operate as a pair to *provoke multiplication* of missional initiatives and churches. Missional engagement, healthy formation, and multiplication are characteristics Communitas would love to see cultivated in all our projects and churches!

Debrief: *We've looked at a real life story of how these dynamics work themselves out in church planting over a number of years. And we've explored more specifics on what the dynamics mean and how they interrelate to one another. Finally, we've noted that the six dynamics can be logically paired along the lines of three distinct purposes - purposes which guide the structure of the next three parts of this book. Before we get into those dynamic pairs, we have another critical issue to unpack with you to help your team be better prepared for the long journey ahead.*

My Reflections:

What did you learn that was new to you?

What worked well for you in this chapter?

What needs to be changed to be more effective for you?

Name two or three standout thoughts. What will you do with these?

How are you currently using what you have experienced in this chapter?

Chapter 2 – Centering Ourselves In Who God Says We Are

 You might feel ready now to jump in - "Hey, let's get started on these dynamics and see what happens!" However, we encourage you to corral that energy for just a while longer, as we need first to deal with a core concept: our identity. Our identity has a lot to do with determining our actions. The inner life of an individual, team, or church eventually leaks out into the outer world - for good or for bad. Where we root our identity can either nourish our souls or it can deplete us of life and joy. Let's look first at our individual identity, then our corporate identity as a team or church.

MY Identity Matters

Stomping through the woods, Kelly began to scream, as loud as he could, at God. Two days into a solitude retreat at a silent monastery in the mountains, ten years of church-planting, and three churches into his effort, Kelly was angry. He had done everything he could think of for God, he had followed all the rules, dedicated his life to ministry, and as far as he could tell, God had done nothing. No success, no new Christians, and Kelly was lonelier than ever. Confused and utterly exhausted, he was done.

So with only cows to hear him, Kelly screamed at God: his soul-shaking disappointment, his anger, his fear. He yelled until he had no words left. In the silence that followed, Kelly audibly heard God ask, "Who am I?" Over the days and

months that followed, he realized that complete intimacy comes only in God, and that God had already validated Kelly's existence by creating him. Kelly had nothing left to do but accept that truth.

Henri Nouwen wrote, "Jesus came to announce to us that an identity based on success, popularity and power is a false identity - it's an illusion! Loudly and clearly Jesus says: 'You are not what the world makes you; but you are children of God.'"[7] Even *good* behav-

---

7   Henri Nouwen, *Here and Now: Living in the Spirit* (New York: Crossroad, 2002), 163.

iors that are motivated by a need to please others, ourselves, or God eventually lead to emptiness or anger. In contrast, receiving and resting in our identity as God's beloved children allows us to be filled by an inner spring that never runs dry.

Before we start ministry we need to examine the source of our identity. And throughout our lives we'll need to periodically revisit this to make sure we're aware of where our motivations are rooted. Is our identity based on the need to gain the praise of our parents or certain authority figures we respect? Are we people-pleasers, ever trying to satisfy the expectations of our friends or to gain praises from the world? Does our sense of self come from the clothes we wear, the rules we follow, the political party we join, or how well we perform at our jobs? Are we striving to prove something to someone, maybe even trying to prove something to ourselves?

Or, are we caught on the treadmill of trying to earn God's approval? This question is particularly important, as it tends to be one we readily excuse as virtuous. Many church planters are secretly plagued with this inner drive to please God, just as Kelly was in the opening story. This can lead to a sense of entitlement - God owes me and my family a payback - and it can lead to a roller coaster ride with God. When our ministry is bearing fruit, we're happy because God must be happy with our results; and when it seems dry and unfruitful despite our hard work, we're unhappy because we conclude that God is withholding blessings from us, that we just don't make the grade, or that we're somehow guilty of doing something displeasing.

Our identity and value in God's eyes never changes. God declares that value in creating us in His image, in giving us life, and in choosing to bear our sin and brokenness so that each one of us might know that we are a precious, adopted child of God. In God's eyes we can never become less valuable, less beloved, or less important. In God's eyes we will never gain more favor, more praise, more perfection than that which we already have through Christ. The primary question we need to come back to again and again is: *Is our sense of self really based in the assurance that God has always and will always love us?* We may superficially answer 'yes' to this question, and yet still harbor deep-seated beliefs that root our value elsewhere. Or we may have once embraced this truth but drifted from that security we once knew in God. Because we see all ministry flowing from the fountain of our God-declared value, we include the following exercise to help you reconnect with the Source who loves us unconditionally.

Staying Grounded in Who God Made Me to Be

Time: 60 minutes
Supplies: Bible, journal, pen or pencil

1. Find a place where you will not be disturbed and take some unrushed time alone with your journal open and your Bible before you. Begin with a prayer that invites the Holy Spirit to help you see yourself as you are and to guide your thoughts.

2. As you sit prayerfully, respond to these prompts in your journal:
    - *When have you felt weak, or experienced failure, suffering, or loss?*
    - *What messages do you tell yourself when this happens?*
    - *What does this tell you about how you attach yourself to and adapt to the world's view of success, power, and self-worth?*
    - *To whom do you go for help?*

3. Sit quietly for a few minutes and allow the Holy Spirit to speak to you. What do you hear or feel? What images come to mind? Jot them down in your journal. When you are ready, respond to the following prompts, noting your responses in your journal:
    - *What are the key verses, stories, metaphors that remind you of who God has made you to be?*
    - *How do these stories, verses, metaphors relate to you personally? Where do you feel that you are lacking?*
    - *What personal spiritual practices would you like to develop to stay grounded in who God has made you to be?*
    - *Who can you ask to help you keep your spiritual practices activated in this busy ministry season ahead?*
    - *Make a plan to ask that person to help you.*

4. End in a prayer of thanksgiving offering the Holy Spirit honor for guiding you in this practice. The next time your team meets, share the details of your spiritual practice plan and any significant insights that you have had about this learning exercise.

OUR Identity Matters

In church planting our identity as the people of God, the church, is as important as our individual identity. How we understand our collective identity as God's family determines our collective actions and ministry. The source of our collective identity determines the quality of our testimony about who God is.

Is our collective identity as a missional initiative or church based on a super-hero view of saving the world? Is it based on a political notion of creating the perfect kingdom? Is our identity shaped by a fear of *them* and the need to protect *us*? Do we see ourselves primarily as a self-help group that exists to make each participant a better and happier individual?

...Or, does our collective identity come from the one true God who deserves all worship and honor? Is our identity grounded in a Trinity who so desperately loves the world that He will go to any lengths for them to know Him? Does it find its moorings in a Mystery who holds justice and mercy, grace and truth in perfect harmony? Is it defined by the great Namer who has called His people to join in freeing His creation from bondage and decay for the goodness of freedom and glory?

"Henri Nouwen pointed out that we find an identity in part through what others say about us. What others say about us can shape our self-identity in profound ways. Identities are not found; they are given. For many of us, identities are given by people who don't have the right to identify us. True identities can be given only by God."[8]

In the Bible, we read what God says about His people. God gives identity to His people through story after story. In the story of creation, "God saw that it was good." He makes men and women as part of this creation and says "all He had made was good."

During the time of Abraham, God renewed His relationship with His people. God called a specific family to be His people, through whom "all the families of the earth will be blessed."[9] God called Abram and named him Abraham, covenanting that through Abraham's obedience, not only he and his family but the entire earth would be blessed.

God called His people, the Israelites - the family of Abraham - out of slavery in Egypt. He empowered them to live into their identity as God's people so that all the nations would see who God is and experience His great love (Deut. 4). The story is told over and over of God's people called out of slavery to live in a land "flowing with milk and honey" where justice and mercy, grace and truth, and true goodness flourished. From Exodus to Malachi, we see God calling His people back time and time again through His prophets to live in obedience, to live into the reality of a good creation, including "a demonstration to the nations that 'there is no other god besides me, a

righteous God and a Saviour... To me every knee shall bow, every tongue shall swear allegiance'

(Is. 45:22-23)."[10]

As the Israelites are sent from their land into exile in Babylon, God enlists Jeremiah to send a message to His people, reminding them of who He is calling them to be (Jer. 29). The Israelites will not be defined by what others say about them (a nation of conquered exiles), but by what God says about them. God says they are free and a chosen people, called to mediate God's grace and character to the world. And despite their present judgment and exile, God continues to remain faithful to His promises to bless them and give them a bright future.

By means of a letter from the prophet Jeremiah, God delivers a message to His exiled people that culminates in a call to live in Babylon in an unexpected way:

"This is what the Lord Almighty, the God of Israel, says to all those I carried into exile from Jerusalem to Babylon: Build houses and settle down; plant gardens and eat what they produce. Marry and have sons and daughters; find wives for your sons and give your daughters in marriage, so that they too may have sons and daughters. Increase in number there; do not decrease. Seek the peace and prosperity of the city to which I have carried you into exile. Pray to the Lord for it, because if it prospers, you too will prosper." - Jeremiah 29:4-7

In their translations of the original Hebrew text, most of our English Bibles mask the presence of a significant word that actually occurs three times in verse seven above. That word is *"shalom."* To highlight Jeremiah's repeated use of *shalom*, Old Testament scholar Walter Brueggemann offers this translation of the original Hebrew:

---

8   David Lomas, *The Truest Thing about You: Identity, Desire, and Why It All Matters* (Colorado Springs: David C. Cook, 2014), 94.

9   Genesis 12:3.

---

10 Andrew Perriman, "Missio Dei in Historical Perspectives, Part 2," http://www.postost.net/2011/01/missio-dei-historical-perspectives-part-2 (accessed 25 May 2015).

*"Seek the **shalom** of the city where I have sent you into exile, pray to the Lord on its behalf, for in its **shalom** you too will find your **shalom**."*[11]

To understand how profound this recurring word must have sounded in the ears of the Hebrew exiles, we need to get beyond the simple non-Hebrew definitions that we tend to project onto that word. In the original Hebrew language of the Old Testament, *shalom* meant so much more than how we typically define it today. Words like peace, prosperity, and well-being capture some aspects of the richer meaning, but their range is too narrow. In the Bible *shalom* means "universal flourishing, wholeness, and delight—a rich state of affairs that inspires joyful wonder as its Creator and Savior opens doors and welcomes the creatures in whom he delights."[12] Walter Brueggemann draws out the communal and societal dimensions of *shalom* by defining it as: "a sense of personal wholeness in a community of justice and caring that addresses itself to the needs of all humanity and all creation."[13] Brueggemann and other biblical scholars also allude to *shalom* as a visionary term - the idea of God's people living now in the direction that God is moving all things. *Shalom* is about the future that's promised, but it's also about what God wants to give us in some measure in the present (consider that Jesus Himself gave us this prayer: "Thy Kingdom come! Thy will be done, on earth as it is in heaven."). These profound meanings are closer to what the Old Testament prophets meant by *shalom*.

---

11 Walter Brueggemann, *Living Toward a Vision: Biblical Reflections on Shalom* (Philadelphia: United Church Press, 1982), 23.

12 Cornelius Plantinga Jr., *Not the Way It's Supposed to Be: A Breviary of Sin* (Grand Rapids: Wm. B. Eerdmans, 1995), 10.

13 This is condensed summary of Brueggemann's definition (see *Living Toward a Vision*, pp. 181-183).

So if you happened to be a Hebrew exile listening to the reading of this letter from Jeremiah, you'd likely be quite surprised to hear *shalom* repeated within a broader message telling your people to put down roots. Instead of promising immediate deliverance, God was actually asking you and your people to shed your negative identities as victims, slaves, or misfits in a foreign land. Instead, you were all called to be missionaries, sent to declare God's reign and to display His goodness. The call was not to withdraw, nor for you to pray for God to rain down judgment upon your captors. You were not being asked to be cancerous agents in society, nor to subversively act in any way to the harm of Babylon. On the contrary, God's message was an invitation for you and your people to embrace a radically different identity in your circumstances: *"You are not captives in your present setting; you are My missionaries of shalom!"*

It's amazing enough that God asked His people to seek the *shalom* of this hostile place, Babylon! But God also lets them know that in their active blessing of Babylon, they too would find *shalom*. Can you imagine how profound this message must have sounded to God's people? To seek the *shalom* of Babylon would mean living among a people who did not know God and also living into that grand purpose God's people have always had (and were prone to forget): to shine forth God's glory and good intentions for the world. While this would be a healing way to live, transformative to both the exiles and to their captors, it would also be costly. For one, they would have to seek the *shalom* of foreigners they certainly hated. How hard it would be to put aside bitterness and to offer forgiveness. Seeking the *shalom* of Babylon would also require the exiles to venture out into this huge city. And it would be disruptive to the systems of evil and injustice in Babylonian society, drawing resistance, and even persecution.

CHAPTER 2

Dynamic Adventure

Part One - The Basics: Packing for the Journey Ahead - 17

With this positive identity crisply etched into their hearts - "We are God's beloved people sent into the world to represent the one true God and portray His *shalom*" - the Jews would have an opportunity over many long years in Babylon to testify that God reigns over the *whole* earth. God's *shalom* reign is active in the farthest away of places, and even in the least expected places.

What a significant story in the unfolding narrative of God's people! Babylon has disappeared into the sands of time, and yet that story rings true for us. Something marvelous has happened in the meantime that changes everything! We, in contrast to God's people in Babylon, stand on the other side of fulfilled prophecy - Messiah Jesus has come, the One whose name is "Prince of *Shalom*!"[14] In and through Jesus, God calls His people, now named the *church*, to live into that new reality. We as God's people today face our own "Babylons" across this earth. And we arguably bear a similar call to seek the *shalom* of all those places, regardless of how daunting and unappealing that call may seem.

Following in the example of Jesus, we proclaim God's reign over the lost and over the unexpected places, where sin and brokenness assert their reign. Using the language of the New Testament era, Christ calls God's people to live into the "Kingdom of God," which is the essence of the *shalom* order God has been moving history towards all along.

Through sermons and parables, Jesus shows time and again that this Kingdom is not like the kingdoms of the world. Contrary to the way of the world, Jesus calls for a community where the meek are blessed, enemies are loved, the first are last, and a mustard seed becomes a great tree.

Paul, Peter, and the apostles take up the language of this call to the church and build upon it. Through their many stories and letters, God reminds His church who they are. God defines them as a community who daringly worship the one true God and who live out a radical reconciliation where there is no separation between Gentile and Jew, slave and owner, male and female.[15] The people of God are to be "a holy people, a royal priesthood" who declare God's wonderful light.[16]

What a wonderful and positive identity we carry into the world as God's people! This is worth our deep reflection. But it requires us to let go of those things that stand in the way of embracing this identity. We need to grieve or lament the losses we may feel, including other emotions that may hinder us in our call, such as anger, fear, or cynicism. This allows us to put on that positive identity God intends us to display in whatever cultural setting we find ourselves. The following exercises are designed to help you and your team take the time to let go of what needs to be shed, and to fully embrace the positive call in culture that God has given you.

---

14   Isaiah 9:6.

15   Galatians 3:28.

16   1 Peter 2:9.

Lamenting a Shared Experience

Time: 60 minutes
Supplies: Journal, pen or pencil, Bible

Any team which engages context in the name of Christ will want to give its members the space to lament. It is important to acknowledge and express grief over how far short both the church and culture have fallen in representing God's *shalom* order. The team needs time to grieve those good things culture has taken away from God's people, from humanity, and creation as a result of the worship of false gods. This expression of lament can help people address emotions that otherwise could hinder them from moving forward in culture with courage and godly optimism.

Take some quiet time alone with the journal section of this chapter and your Bible. Slowly work through the following exercises, journaling your thoughts.

1. Open your Bible to Jeremiah 29:4-7. As you read God's message to the exiles, imagine what the captives would have been hearing and feeling. There was so much about their day-to-day existence that changed.
   - *How was Babylonian culture pulling or chafing at their identity?*
   - *Is your own culture chafing against you as a person of faith?*
   - *In your journal list a few ways that you are feeling chafed by your cultural setting, ways that you feel bogged down.*
   - *Compare and contrast the exiles experience with yours.*

2. Israel lamented her captivity. Read Psalms 6, 137, and 22. Psalm 22 starts out with "My God, my God, why have you forsaken me?" It ends with "It is finished."[17] Jesus was likely singing Psalm 22 as He suffered and died on the cross.[18] Many of the Psalms are laments. A lament allows one to grieve before God. No emotion is off limits or unholy, but is freely expressed before God. What surprises you about these psalms you just read? What emotions do you relate to?

3. As an exile in Babylon you would likely have lamented the prophetic words of Jeremiah to stay, pray for, and seek the *shalom* of the Babylonians.
   - *What causes you to lament in your own context?*
   - *Write your own psalm of lament describing your experience with your context/captivity.*

4. Post your lament somewhere in your home where it will remind you to recite it to God.

---

17 Matt. 27:46.
18 John 19:30.

Embracing Shalom

Time: 30-60 minutes
Supplies: Bible, journal, pens or pencils

1. With a discussion partner name as many Bible stories or passages that tell about God's work to usher in God's *shalom* reign in Bible times. Are there any other metaphors besides *shalom* which describe this new order? Note them on a fresh page in your journal.

2. Tell your partner of a time that you have seen God's *shalom* reign faithfully expressed in culture. Describe a situation where you found *shalom* in a person you least expected (e.g. through a non-Christian friend or group, etc.). Note these in your journal.

3. Gathering as a team, each person shares first about their partner's experience of *shalom* in culture and then in an unexpected person.

4. The facilitator guides the team to compare and contrast the experiences of *shalom* in scripture to the current day examples that have been shared. Use the questions below to prompt the discussion:
   • *How are the scripture examples and our current experiences similar?*
   • *How are they different?*
   • *What do these experiences lead you to expect from God?*
   • *How is the Holy Spirit prompting you personally to action?*

5. The facilitator leads the team to consider the following statement: Imagine God asking you to be a missionary of *shalom*.
   • *What does it feel like to assume that identity?*
   • *How might it affect your attitude and actions as you engage daily life within your local setting?*

6. Note the team's responses in your journal for further contemplation, conversation, and action.

God's story for His people has not ended. He continues to tell our stories and name His people as people of His new creation. In Jesus, God gives us our true identity. Becoming God's people is no longer defined by being of Abraham's blood, or even the covenant sign of circumcision, but by trusting in Jesus as Savior and Lord.[19] The people of God live in His Kingdom where *shalom*-filled new creation breaks into this present order. This unfolding reality is coming in fullness at the return of the King, but

_____

19 Romans 4, Galatians 3.

even now God's people point to the new creation and its *shalom*. This has tremendous implications for the way we approach culture!

Author Andy Crouch claims we as Christians tend to adopt negative or reactive postures toward the culture we're immersed in. He has identified four basic postures or stances American Christians over the past two centuries have adopted toward culture, which we capture in the diagram below. Crouch is speaking primarily to the American church, and yet

we find these postures applicable on some level to Christians in any cultural setting.[20] As you read them consider how they might apply to your context.

---

20 Andy Crouch, *Culture Making: Recalling our Creative Calling* (Downers Grove: InterVarsity Press, 2013), 60-74. Reinhold Niebuhr wrote a classic text on this as well called *Christ and Culture*, while Tim Keller also identifies different models of cultural engagement in *Center Church*.

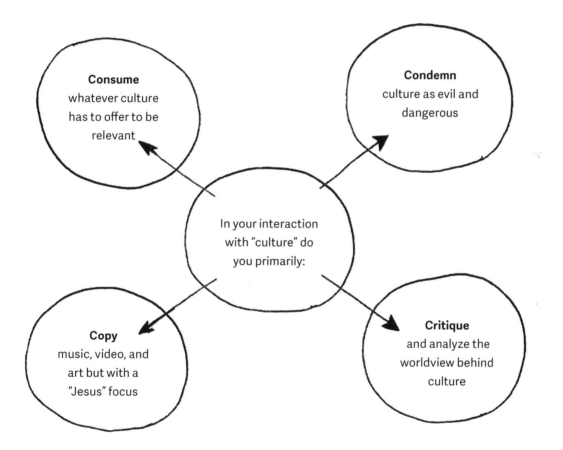

To live into the positive identity God has given us, both as His beloved children and as His missional people, we need to evaluate the postures we tend to take toward our host culture. How we behave has huge potential implications for the gospel! The

following exercise is designed to help your team identify any negative or unfruitful postures you may be harboring, including how you might replace those with a better, more positive way to operate within your cultural setting.

Discerning and Implementing More Positive Responses to Culture

Time: 60 minutes
Supplies: Journal and pen or pencil

1. Examine the chart above. How do you resonate with these postures? Circle what seems familiar to you. If you do not resonate with these, write in your journal those areas of culture that are difficult for you to understand or accept, or those to which you have a negative response. Circle your top one or two negative responses either in the above diagram or in your journal.

2. Read the section below where Crouch offers two alternative postures the church might adopt in its cultural settings. Underline those words and phrases that are significant to you.

    The postures of artists and gardeners have a lot in common. Both begin with contemplation, paying close attention to what is already there. The gardener looks carefully at the landscape; the existing plants, both flowers and weeds; the way the sun falls on the land. The artist regards her subject, her canvas, her paints with care to discern what she can make with them.

    And then, after contemplation, the artist and gardener both adopt a posture of purposeful work. They bring their creativity and effort to their calling. Why aren't we known as cultivators - people who tend and nourish what is best in human culture, who do the hard painstaking work to preserve the best of what people before us have done? Why aren't we known as creators - people who dare to think and do something that has never been thought or done before, something that makes the world more welcoming and thrilling and beautiful?[21]

3. On a fresh page in your journal (left hand side of the page), note any negative postures you tend to have toward culture, including the ones you may have circled in the diagram above. Now, on the right hand side of the page write the words and phrases that you underlined in the quote above. They should be fairly contrasting in nature. If you are like most folks, you would have underlined words like *contemplation, artists* and *gardeners, creators* and *cultivators.* You may have underlined verbs such as *nourish, paying attention, dare to think, welcoming,* etc.

4. Write a reflection about your negative posture towards culture responding to these prompts:
    *   *Name what it is that irritates you about culture. Then use as many of the terms that you under-lined in the second section to suggest to yourself ways that you might develop a different posture.*
    *   *How will you look beyond that which bothers you?*
    *   *How will you build a positive relationship to culture? Include a few of Crouch's concepts that you have underlined.*
    *   *Tell how you will become an artist or a gardener in your context.*

---

21 Crouch, *Culture Making,* 97-98.

5. End your journal entry with a paragraph written to the culture about your resolve and commitment to love it. Make a date to share your reflection with your mentor.

Culture is not something that is beyond, against, or outside us as God's people. Instead, we inhabit culture as both creators who add positive accents that may be missing, and also as cultivators who improve upon the good that is already there. We join God in this creating and cultivating work, in the power of His Spirit, and in the knowledge of who He has called us to be. Through living into these postures, we contribute to seeing God's desired shalom-filled reality emerge. N.T. Wright says of the people of God, "Our task in the present...is to live as resurrection people in between Easter and the final day, with our Christian life, corporate and individual, in both worship and mission, as a sign of the first and a foretaste of the second."[22] Much of what we explore in this guidebook is intended to help us deepen and live out that new identity as a sign and foretaste, reflectively and communally.

---

22 N.T. Wright, *Surprised by Hope: Rethinking Heaven, the Resurrection, and the Mission of the Church* (New York: HarperCollins, 2008), 30.

Debrief: *In this chapter we have probed deeply into both our personal and communal identity, including how that works itself out in our postures toward culture. We've done this because identity has so many consequences for both our personal well-being and the way we project ourselves in the worlds in which we move. Centering ourselves in who God says we are and keeping that identity intact is one of the most important aspects of our discipleship in Christ. Losing sight of this under the demands of missional church planting can steal away the freedom God invites teams to embrace.*

My Reflections:

What did you learn that was new to you?

What worked well for you in this chapter?

What needs to be changed to be more effective for you?

Name two or three standout thoughts. What will you do with these?

How are you currently using what you have experienced in this chapter?

PART TWO – GOING LOCAL: MOVING IN AND LIVING OUT

Now that we've given you a big-picture view of both our approach to church planting and our identity as God's people, it's time to dig in and explore the first two dynamics: **embed** *and* **initiate**. *The two dynamics work together to activate our missional DNA - that inner core of our missionary calling and its expression outward.* **Embed** *and* **initiate** *are important startup dynamics for missional church, but they need to be continually cultivated throughout the life of any healthy church.*

Chapter 3 - Embed: Getting Inside the Soul of our City

 It's time to roll up our sleeves and dig into **embedding!** *Embedding is a primary missionary team activity that allows us to go deep into our context to see and hear what it's all about. We'll explore the missionary lifestyle and its three interwoven strands:* **Absorb, Relate,** *and* **Serve.** *We'll thoroughly investigate those strands and show you how they weave together to form a pattern of living symbolized by a Celtic Knot. Finally, we'll help you respond to your* **embedding** *by guiding you to discover your SHAPE - your gifts, passions, abilities, personality, and experience - and how to match your SHAPE with the needs you unearth in your context.*

EMBED - *root in context and relational networks as an enriching presence*

What *Embedding* Means and Why it's So Important

In missional church planting, teams must be extra careful to do the crucial work of rooting in the host context, befriending people, and serving long enough to be an enriching presence. Learning to love the people we settle among requires that we gain deep understanding of who they are, how they conduct their daily lives, and what challenges they face. Unfortunately, many church planting initiatives pay little regard to such 'details.' Communitas describes this long cultivating work with the action word *embed*. *Embedding* is important because it provides teams with the critical insights, relationships, and opportunities that provide inroads for the gospel. In this chapter we want to help your team grapple with the *embedding* dynamic. Let's begin with a brief description:

Embedding is about submerging deeply into context and establishing a stable, long-term presence together. Team members, individually and collectively, engage in a missionary lifestyle. This lifestyle involves giving continual attention to three primary behaviors: 1) ABSORBING: listening and learning as much as possible about the city or target area; 2) RELATING: building relationships in natural ways with non-Christians while also relating to Christians who may want to join or partner with the team; and 3) SERVING: participating with both non-Christian and Christian groups in *shalom*-sowing activities and compassion/justice initiatives. By steadfastly exercising these missionary behaviors, a team deepens its awareness of the surrounding culture and its needs. It also begins to grow meaningful relationships with many different kinds of people. And it engages in a growing range of service opportunities.

Over time the team becomes *cultural insiders* who are not only conversant on issues that concern the city but are also responsive to the city's good news, brokenness, and pain. The missionary lifestyle practiced by the core team is continually passed on to others through repeated cycles of modeling, inspiring, and equipping people. This includes a robust immersion in and obedience to our scriptural call to be "in but not of the world."

In the following story, see if you resonate with the importance of getting rooted in context and what that has meant for this group that eventually grew into Emmaus Road Church in Minneapolis, Minnesota. Here's how founding pastor Christine Osgood describes that vital activity in the life of her community:

When our little mission group had grown to 24 people, few if any of us were thinking of forming ourselves into a church.

We were simply a band of people committed to journeying together and living out what it means to follow Jesus. Most of us embraced the idea that our lives needed to show a glimpse of the kingdom to the increasingly postmodern setting around us. However, nearly all of us had spent our entire lives holed up inside the walls of various churches, "living out our faith" in the confines of "the Christian bubble" (i.e. the subculture of American Evangelical Christianity). How in the world were we going to contextualize the good news so that our neighbors could actually hear it and receive it?

We began with baby steps. Week after week we'd gather as a community and challenge each other to venture out or to think differently about the world outside the doors of conventional church. One week, we'd challenge each other to get out into our contexts and listen for God's signature in the story of a person we encountered. Another week we'd challenge each other to move through the week envisioning every person we met as made in the image of God. Still another week we'd encourage each other to serve a person in our neighborhood in a way that would depict Jesus' love for them. As we walked into these challenges from week to week, it began to change us, including how we interacted in our everyday contexts.

As each of us, individually, began to live life differently, we began to notice shifts in our thinking. We were no longer hiding or afraid of our neighbors. Instead, we were eager to engage them and their stories. We began to pray for our neighbors and to listen for ways in which God was moving in their lives. We also found ourselves choosing to spend our free time in different ways. Conviction gripped us as we realized how self-absorbed we all had been. Slowly, the truth of Jesus' way of life began to transform each of us. Life was fuller and more abundant as we lived in ways Christ might well have lived in these neighborhoods, were He to be here bodily today.

Activities like Feed My Starving Children, painting hallways in transitional housing for the homeless, making sandwiches for distribution to those on the streets, making dressers for families coming out of poverty, these were the activities that we began to corporately engage in. A guiding question for us was: "Would this activity align with the missio Dei (the mission of God as laid out in the biblical narrative)?" In our interacting with the Bible and other writings in this season of exploring and experimenting, we had come to see that God's mission in the world was the main thrust of Jesus' lifestyle and ministry. And we were catching glimpses that suggested this mission was everywhere in the storyline of the entire Bible. So if we discerned that an activity was consistent with God's mission in the world, we decided we would engage in that activity.

The exercise below will help develop your understanding of embedding and guide you to consider how to embed in your own context.

Toward a Deeper Understanding of Embedding

Time: 30 minutes
Supplies: Journal and pen or pencil

1. Based on the description of what it means for a team to *embed*, discuss with a partner the words or phrases in the above story that suggest Christine's group was *embedding* well.

2. Compare and contrast Emmaus Road's *embedding* strategy with your own team's *embedding* strategy and experience. How are your experiences similar? What is different?

3. Tell why you think *embedding* is so important on the road to planting a church, including why it is essential to continue *embedding* throughout the life of any church.

4. Name two actions that you will personally do to *embed* well. Write them in the journal section at the end of this chapter.

Author and missiologist Alan Hirsch often makes the point that Christology ought to lead to missiology, which in turn ought to determine ecclesiology. What he means is that our interaction over the life and teachings of Jesus ought to inspire and propel us outward into the world. As we move outward as sent-ones, we root ourselves in the soil of our local settings. This enables us to identify with and get inside the soul of our city. Our missionary work over time ought to naturally inform and shape our ideas of what kind of church may ultimately be needed for our unique setting.

Hirsch argues that teams endeavoring to church plant too easily get the flow of the last two of these backwards. They put ecclesiology before missiology, meaning they determine the form of church before they've done the long missiological work of listening, relating, and serving in context. This often results in the body of Christ huddling like a club for members only, rather than as the embodied presence of Jesus moving into their city. The aim in church planting is not to pool a group of Christians together and move that Christian subculture outwards with a preconceived, ideal model of church. The aim is to immerse ourselves in our local setting and allow this exposure to contour the church culture and model that we're developing.

When groups predetermine the kind of church an area needs before becoming cultural insiders, the chances are high that they will not see many local unchurched people involved in their church. This is especially true where the surrounding culture is vastly different than the internal culture of the church. Some churches recruit and do evangelism well enough to bring in outsiders; but when there's little regard for missionary engagement of context, the people coming in often become so socialized into the subculture of the church that they end up having fewer and fewer significant relationships with anyone outside the church. Even when a team is starting something new in a cultural group similar to their own, they are wise to stay open and continually learn from those around them.

So, starting with a predetermined church model in mind is not the best approach. Instead our missionary work in context gives us an early read on the specific church form most suited to the people we encounter. *Embedding* takes time but is well worth it. With context-appropriate forms of church, more people can find their way toward Jesus Christ, and those churches, whether new or established, can more effectively sow God's *shalom*.

Sowing God's *Shalom*

As we read the stories about Jesus and His values, we see that He loved the idea of the upside-down kingdom: If you want to be the greatest, become a servant. If you want blessing, give away what you have. If someone has wronged you, freely give compassion and forgiveness. Jesus frequently taught His followers to "turn the other cheek," "go the extra mile," and "give him your cloak also."

It is not difficult to find this same pattern in the Old Testament. In Jeremiah's account of the Babylonian exile, Israel was stripped of all that was holy to them. Their hearts were heavy, and they were a broken people. As we noted earlier, the prophet encouraged them to *act* as if they were the ones sent to bring *shalom* to their captors. At that point in their desperation, all the Israelites wanted was a deliverer. They wanted good news... and they got it. That news just wasn't in the "language" that they could readily understand. God was asking them to behave in a counter-instinctive manner, to act in the opposite spirit to what they were naturally inclined to do in such terrible circumstances.

This is the upside-down kingdom at work. As the exiles obeyed and served in Babylon, blessing would come their way. If they did not obey, they would perish. The stakes were high. As a missionary people, the stakes are high for us too. In the following exercise we will revisit the story of Israel in exile in order to help you imagine practical ways to sow *shalom* in your own context.

Discovering and Seeking Shalom *for Your Context*

Time: 45 minutes

Supplies: Bible, large sheets of paper, markers, journal, pens or pencils

1. In small groups, a volunteer reads aloud Jeremiah 29:4-7. As you listen, contemplate what this message must have meant for the Israelites. What emotions would have been normal in this situation? What adjustments would they have had to make in their thoughts and attitudes?

   "This is what the LORD Almighty, the God of Israel, says to all those I carried into exile from Jerusalem to Babylon: Build houses and settle down; plant gardens and eat what they produce. Marry and have sons and daughters; find wives for your sons and give your daughters in marriage, so that they too may have sons and daughters. Increase in number there; do not decrease. Also, seek the peace and prosperity of the city to which I have carried you into exile. Pray to the LORD for it, because if it prospers, you too will prosper."

   - Jeremiah 29:4-7

2. List other Bible characters that found themselves risking their lives to bring blessing to their oppressors. There are quite a few in the Old Testament. Each brought *shalom* to their context in a unique way. As your group discusses these people, note the obstacles that they had to overcome as well as any other themes that you observe.

3. Now think about your own context. Discuss with your group the obstacles you must conquer to be sowers of *shalom*. Compare yourself to the Bible characters you listed in step two. How do you differ? How are you similar?

4. Taking the lead from Jeremiah 29:4-7, name the specific actions the exiles were instructed to take to *embed* in Babylon. What would the exiles have had to do to follow through with those instructions? (For example, "planting a garden" would have required them to learn what crops grow in Babylon, where to get the seeds/plants, what are the growth seasons, etc.) Discuss how those actions might relate to your own *embedding* in context.

5. On a large sheet of paper draw images of actions you could take to *embed* in your context for the sake of sowing *shalom*.

6. Gather together as a team. Each group takes turns explaining their images and actions to the team. Compile a list of actions and record them in your journal, as you will need them for future exercises.

As revealed in the exercise above, God's people likely had to take many additional actions to *embed* in Babylon beyond what is recorded in Jeremiah's letter. What appear to be simple and straight-forward commands, such as "build houses" or "plant gardens," would have caused them to engage in a great deal of missionary activity. The information, connections, and resources they discovered along the way would be critical to fulfilling their call to sow *shalom* in their new home. As missionaries seeking to *embed* well and bring God's *shalom* in our present day situation, we face similar challenges that demand a prolonged, multi-layered response.

What Good Missionaries Do and Have Always Done: A Simple Pattern for Local Embedding

If we tried to describe all the missionary behaviors necessary to be fruitful sowers of God's shalom, we'd probably end up with a list that could be a book in itself. The aim, however, is not to busy ourselves with as many activities as we can imagine, but to pace ourselves and wisely engage our city. Toward that end we want to explore a practical paradigm with you that we believe can: a) help your team get a clearer grasp of missionary living in a balanced, sustainable manner; and b) equip your team with a simple-to-explain visual pattern to help others in your community easily grasp and also activate this lifestyle.

The sketch below (see figure 1) illustrates a simple pattern of missionary living that is proving helpful in many settings.[23] The pattern describes normal behaviors practiced by missionaries as they embed and incarnate Christ within any given cultural group.

---

23 This paradigm was developed by Dan Steigerwald and is more extensively described in his book, *Growing Local Missionaries* (Portland: Urban Loft Publishers, 2014).

Figure 1 - The Missionary Lifestyle
(A Non-linear Pattern Involving Three Pairs of Behavior)

Immerse & Listen = **ABSORBING**

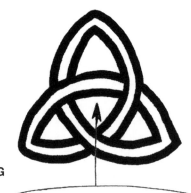

Connect and Befriend = **RELATING**   Participate and Enrich = **SERVING**

GOD & THE BODY OF CHRIST
(Our Center of Discernment & Enablement)

As you see, the pattern above is defined by three pairs of action. Each pair contains two present tense verbs, and the singular words in CAPITAL letters represent the end purpose that is in view as those actions are carried out. Effective missionaries will inevitably practice these three behaviors as they engage a local context. In doing so, they will achieve three beautiful purposes at an increasing depth:

1. *Immerse and Listen* = ABSORBING
2. *Connect and Befriend* = RELATING
3. *Participate and Enrich* = SERVING

When a missionary team first engages a context, a natural sequence of these behaviors unfolds. But they quickly give way to a repeating, overlapping cycle. When missionaries *embed* in a given setting, they must first immerse and listen, *absorbing* as much as they can about their target area. Observing and the taking in of critical information quickly move into *relating* or connecting with locals and those who are "in-the-know" about the area. Slowly over time, the *relating* leads to the building of a smaller subset of meaningful friendships. At the same time the connecting involves choices to *serve* with local people in worthy causes or activities consistent with enriching the city. In other words, any initial sequence in the outworking of these behaviors soon gives way to a continuous, non-sequential engagement in all the missionary activities. With conscious attention to integrating these behaviors into daily life, they become habits individuals and groups learn to practice, almost unconsciously.

We use the Celtic Knot above to visually capture and teach the ongoing, seamless nature of these behaviors in the lifestyle of missionaries. Take your finger and follow the line through the knot. You'll see that it's continuous and overlapping, just as the rhythm of our missionary behaviors ought to be.

By using the Celtic Knot, we are also able to emphasize the importance of ongoing dialogue with God and our spiritual community while practicing each pair of behaviors. In our diagram we designate the center of intersection of the lines as the *center of discernment*, since all our missionary actions are done in ongoing dialogue with God and with our spiritual community. Throughout the course of our missionary behaviors we're continually passing through the center of discernment asking: What do God and my community have to say about what I am *absorbing*? Who I am *relating* to? and, Where I am *serving*? In the next chapter we'll talk more about the importance of communal discernment and how teams might exercise it.

The beauty of the Celtic Knot is its simplicity. The image itself and the behaviors it represents are highly reproducible. We encourage you to review with your team the meaning of each of the pairs of missionary behavior below. Then dig into the learning exercises, which are designed to help you apply each of the behaviors to your context.

Immerse and Listen (*Absorbing*) as Missionary Behavior

Description: Our team must indwell our context in a deep and enduring way. This requires us to cultivate the discipline of sustained curiosity. We must get below the surface of our context, and then, like a high-capacity sponge, take in as much as we can about our surroundings. *Absorbing* includes learning about the values, norms, and history of local culture, including the languages and symbols people use. To deepen our discovery and get down to details we might otherwise miss, we ask many clarifying questions. We also note the social rhythms of the people, and pay close attention to the stories of those we're encountering. These stories give us priceless insights into what's really happening in our context. Over time, by immersing and listening on an increasingly broader and deeper level, we begin to discover the assets, opportunities, gifts, and talents that we as a team can build on and bless.

The next exercise is designed to help you immerse and listen in your context.

Understanding Absorbing *as a Primary Missionary Behavior*

Time: 45 minutes
Supplies: Journal, whiteboard and markers, pens or pencils

1. In the gathering of the larger team the facilitator reviews the above description of *absorbing* and the following examples of contextual questions related to *absorbing*:
   - *What is good news to the people God has placed us among?*
   - *Where is God already at work in our city and our specific area?*
   - *Where have people been impacted by the lament, pain, and the sins of the neighborhood and city? What do they consider to be bad news?*
   - *How do people who don't follow Jesus feel about Christians? The Church? What do you think keeps them away from God?*

2. Take turns sharing meaningful experiences of how you have participated in *absorbing* or how you have observed others practicing it well. What are some of the important contextual questions that these experiences of *absorbing* helped answer? Is there anything about *absorbing* that you don't understand?

3. Each person records in their journal the *absorbing* questions they feel are most relevant to the team. These questions might come from the stories shared, the list in step one, or an important idea not yet mentioned.

4. Each teammate shares with the team their top three *absorbing* questions. Facilitator writes them on the whiteboard.

5. Decide as a team the top three *absorbing* questions you would like to seek answers for in your context. Discuss initial actions you will take to answer those questions. Make a simple plan to implement those actions.

As missionaries, the neighborhood is one of the sacred texts we must learn to read. There are many ways to *absorb* information about our context, ranging from simple attentiveness in daily life to focused research projects. The practice of neighborhood exegesis in the exercise below is a great way to immerse and listen to your context. We encourage you to get your friends, both Christian and non-Christian, involved and on their feet in a regular rhythm of listening together. Another similar practice is the ministry of Peripateo described in Appendix B.

Listening and Learning Via Neighborhood Exegesis

Time: 3 to 4 hours
*Supplies: maps with enough different walking routes to accommodate your team, access to Appendix C (either print it out or take this book with you). **You will also need to find a resident from the neighborhood to engage in your group discussion***

What is neighborhood exegesis? The word *exegesis* means literally *reading out*. It is normally used as a theological term describing the activity of digging into the background, history, ethos, and literary context of a passage of Scripture. When we apply this to a given area of our city, *neighborhood exegesis* is the activity of digging into the background, history, ethos, and contextual issues of a particular area or people group. It is a thorough *reading out* of a given context to discover what's really there.

Neighborhood exegesis is not a demographic study conducted with minimal investment in real relationships with locals. Instead, it provides a means by which a church or church planting team can increase its awareness and responsiveness to those it is called to reach and serve. Participants will find this practice stimulating, fun, and informative - all at the same time! And if it is included as a regular spiritual practice for your team, it can lead to a growing bounty of information and relationships in your city. As you plan for the time you will do the exercise, ask someone you know who lives in the area to come and join you.

1. In groups of four or less, pray and ask God to give you ears to hear and eyes to see what is happening in the area you are about to walk. Choose a route in a different direction for each group, and plan to set out on foot for at least an hour. Now, go to Appendix C and follow the instructions for the Neighborhood Exegesis Exercise. When you return from your adventure, use the following questions to debrief your experience with your group of fellow explorers:
    *   *What did I notice in myself as I walked this part of the city – thoughts, questions, strong feelings, or reactions, etc.?*
    *   *What stood out to us in particular?*
    *   *Rehearse the story of your relic, and identify who will tell the story about it.*

2. Come back together as a team. Take turns sharing your group's impressions and responses to the above questions. Each group ends their sharing by talking about how the relic or symbol represents your group's experience of walking the community.

3. After each small group has shared with the team, discuss these questions:
   - *What signs of* shalom *did you note? Where did you notice God already at work?*
   - *What might it look like to "seek the shalom" of this part of the city?*
   - *What are the questions that emerge from your exposure to the area?*
   - *What were the themes that emerged in your conversations with people? What appears to be important to them - what questions are they asking?*

4. After responding to the above questions, invite the local resident from the community to comment on what was heard:
   - *How accurate is our portrayal of the area?*
   - *What is missing that was not observed that's not so obvious, or only things a resident of the area might see?*

5. Then, invite the resident to tell you a personal version of the story of this neighborhood. Ask "open questions" to learn more about this area of the city. Look in Appendix D if you are unfamiliar with open questions.

 ## Connect and Befriend (*Relating*) as Missionary Behavior

Description: As we immerse and listen and patiently wring out greater understanding from our context, we're beginning to meet a variety of people. This direct human contact is likely our greatest source of helpful knowledge and insights about our city. While accessing the insider knowledge of local Christians can be beneficial, as missionaries our priority is to connect and eventually befriend those who've yet to meet Jesus. Some of these connections will come easily as we encounter people frequently or find that they are open and friendly toward us. Over time, as these relationships are cultivated, some people will readily reveal more and more about their personal hopes, fears, pain, and biases. They move beyond sharing information about the city or neighborhood and let us into their lives. This is sacred ground.

In order to benefit from this gift of vulnerable sharing, we must not only prioritize being around people but also be genuinely interested, available, and willing to engage in unhurried conversations. Some of our repeated connections will naturally grow into meaningful exchanges, and if we are patient, friendships will begin to grow.

In the normal give and take of healthy, growing relationships, we will discover invitations and opportunities to share the good news of Jesus. Over time our friends will share their personal philosophy of life, their hopes, their dreams, and what's good news to them. That's what friends do. But in all this *relating*, we must be careful to steward these relationships with no-strings-attached. People can tell if we have other motives, if we're secretly manipulating them, or if we are viewing them as "projects." We must practice a *do no harm* stance. The person at the other end of our mission must never be belittled, made to feel less than, or shamed. They must be respected as equals with dignity and given credit for their decisions about their own lives. In the end, they are the experts of their own journey. Missionaries must commit themselves to the long work of assimilating into context as insiders with the conviction that the Holy Spirit will begin the work of spiritual awakening at the right time for each person. Mission is about them, not about you.

For our team, connecting and befriending will mean we join or establish various special interest groups with non-Christians, as these provide natural spheres for relationships to grow. We will also want to inhabit popular community spaces or events where locals hang out. As we get in the habit of *relating* to people, we will want to be attentive to finding answers to the kinds of questions in the exercise below.

Understanding Relating *as a Missionary Behavior*

Time: 45 minutes

Supplies: Whiteboard and markers, journal, pens or pencils

1. In the gathering of the larger team the facilitator reviews the above description of relating and reads aloud the sample questions below about *relating* naturally to people in your context:
    *   *How do I start on the road to building true friendships with non-Christians?*
    *   *Who can I identify in my network of people that I might like to spend time with, or who show interest in my life?*
    *   *How do these people intersect with the lives of others on my team, in terms of interests and natural connections?*
    *   *How will I know if my voice is accepted within the community? What are the signs of acceptance?*
    *   *How might we as a team create belonging spaces for non-Christians open to spirituality but not open to coming to a worship gathering?*

2. Take turns sharing meaningful experiences of how you have participated in *relating* or how you have observed others practicing it well. What are some of the important contextual questions that these experiences of *relating* helped answer? Is there anything about *relating* that you don't understand?

3. Each person records in their journal the *relating* questions they feel are most relevant to the team. These questions might come from the stories shared, the list in step one, or an important idea not yet mentioned.

4. Each teammate shares with the team their top three *relating* questions. Facilitator writes them on the whiteboard.

5. Decide as a team the top three *relating* questions you would like to seek answers for in your context. Discuss initial actions you will take to answer those questions. Make a simple plan to implement those actions.

Networks are the most natural avenue that we have for *relating* to people in our context. According to author Michael Frost, our ability to engage with the missional context depends primarily upon three elements: *proximity*, *frequency*, and *spontaneity*.[24] These aspects are leveraged most naturally through our own networks. When these are present, the missionary team has a greater potential for developing natural relationships that can evolve into friendships. We're not suggesting that we develop or *use* friendships primarily to elicit "golden moments" to share our faith. If opportunities to share Christ arise naturally in conversation, that's great, but staying in relationship with friends over the long haul is arguably consistent with the gospel we bring, regardless of how people respond. We explore evangelism in the midst of befriending in the next chapter on the *initiate* dynamic.

Proximity involves relational closeness and physical nearness, essential ingredients in missionary living. Michael Frost writes, "[I]f we take the incarnation seriously, we must take seriously the call to live incarnationally -- right up close, near to those whom God desires to redeem. We cannot demonstrate Christlikeness from a distance from those whom we feel called to serve. We need to get close enough to people that our lives rub up against their lives, and

that they see the incarnated Christ in our values, beliefs, and practices as expressed in cultural forms that make sense and convey impact."[25]

Frequency is necessary to establish meaningful relationships. Our own networks provide ample opportunity for missionary teams to encounter those we wish to reach on a regular basis. There is something about showing up consistently and being present that creates an atmosphere of trust. Frequency leads to familiarity, and a familiar face is always welcomed. Networks often form along lines of need, convenience, ritual, and celebration. This reality allows us to have frequent contact with those who we wish to engage. It allows us to come near to them as well. Think about the coffee shop that you pass each day on your morning walk - do you know the staff or the regulars? Do you know the mail person who walks to *your* house every day? Frequency and proximity are interrelated. Physical nearness often provides opportunity for relational closeness through frequency of contact.

Spontaneity requires a little more work. It demands that we not only value people but that we also become more adaptive with our schedules. In Western culture, this is not always so easy to do, since the hidden message we receive every day is "stay busy and be productive, 24/7." With little critical

---

24 Michael Frost, *Exiles: Living Missionally in a Post-Christian Culture* (Peabody: Hendrickson, 2006), 54-64.

25 Ibid., 55.

reflection we pack our schedules full of commitments from the moment we wake up until bedtime. We spend our days in a hurried frenzy largely of our own making. Yet, think about the routine tasks of life: pumping fuel for the car, buying groceries, mailing packages, riding the bus home from work, engaging with the parents of your children's friends. Each of these ordinary activities provides moments for spontaneity, and thus opportunities for relationship. Without allowing margins of time in our lives these relationships are not possible - we don't have *time*.

Imagine if we as missionaries lived life with a 20% margin. What if 20% of our time was not scheduled but was intentionally left open for spontaneous engagement? How would that change our ability to make relationships, to build friendships?! Our relationship to time is so important we've included a bonus exercise in Appendix E.

The following exercise is meant to be an aid to fostering the elements of proximity, frequency, and spontaneity in order to see relationships grow naturally.

Building Relationships Through Proximity, Frequency, and Spontaneity

Time: 2 Hours; One hour to diagram your work, and another hour to meet with your mentor for evaluation
Supplies: Cardstock, markers, journal, pen or pencil

1. Examining your life in your local setting, consider your relationships in terms of needs you have, celebrations you experience, rituals you participate in, and convenience you seek. On a sheet of cardstock, write down as many of these as you can. For example: Facebook, daycare, school programs, Pilates class, Halloween, bank, coffee shop, etc. These are your relationships of proximity.

2. On another sheet of cardstock make a second list of the networks that overlap. For example, you may see the same person at the coffee shop and at the bus stop. Also think about the networks you routinely participate in. Do you see the same people at your child's daycare every day? Are you a 'regular' at the gym? These are your relationships of frequency. Who do you see there and how often? How might these relationships provide context and opportunity for mission? Post your diagrams either inside the cover of your Bible or at your desk where you can see them regularly. Begin praying for those whom you wish to engage more deeply.

3. Design a simple plan to maximize your influence within one of your networks. You might choose a celebration, a ritual, a need, or a convenience that allows you easy access to the network. This could be a walk, interviews, regularly planned celebrations, hanging out at a pub, giving things away, or whatever else your imagination can come up with. In your journal, describe your plan and how you expect it to increase your relational connections.

4. Execute your plan. Journal your impressions. What worked well? What did not work? What could you have done differently? Evaluate your results with your mentor.

One of the most effective ways to learn what is happening in a culture is to find an insider, someone who has enough history and stake in the city to really know the good, the bad, and the ugly. We call this person a "cultural advocate." A good advocate can increase our knowledge of context better than almost any other person or means.

Enlisting a Cultural Advocate

Time: 3 to 4 hours
Supplies: Journal, pen or pencil

1. Read the description below of a cultural advocate. Underline what stands out to you.

   To better understand a culture or context that is new to you, you will need to find a cultural insider, someone who is willing to come alongside you to interpret what you are observing and experiencing. That person needs to be someone who likes you, wants to help you grow, and is willing to take the time to meet with you regularly. And, of course, you must have enough of a common language to make this plausible. This person will become a helpful advocate as you observe and make sense of cultural norms, beliefs, superstitions, religion, family practices, kinship groups, etc.

   Your advocate should be a truth teller and not simply a person who repeats back to you what she thinks you want to hear. The more honest she is, the more likely you will learn what you need to know. Often older folks and teenagers are very good candidates because they tend to have more time. Your advocate must be capable of understanding you and evaluating your projects and ideas for legitimacy, for what will work within the cultural setting you're in. She will help you understand what works and what does not.

   Take care in deciding who your advocate will be. It helps if you choose a person of your faith, but that is not necessary. Your relationship with your advocate will ideally be long standing. You are the learner in this relationship. If your advocate is not a follower of Jesus, do not attempt to evangelize him. You will likely lose him if you do so. Be sure to show appreciation by treating him to a coffee or a lunch. Make it worth his time, as much as you can. Thank him profusely!

2. What questions do you have about a cultural advocate? Discuss them with your mentor.

3. Brainstorm a list of potential advocates. Meet with your mentor and develop a few open questions (see Appendix D) to ask of your potential advocates.

4. Choose a few candidates who could become your advocate and interview them with the open questions. Evaluate your interviews and decide whom you would like to ask to journey with you.

5. Make an appointment and invite that person into a friendship as your advocate. Bring a few open questions to ask your advocate about the culture. Allow these questions to be situations or customs that you truly do not understand. Describe to this person what you have already learned about the culture. Ask him which of your perceptions ring true and which do not. Listen and learn. Allow yourself to be corrected and allow your heart to be changed.

6. As a point of accountability and an opportunity to deepen your learning, report back to your mentor what you have gained as a result of your first meeting with your advocate.

Participate and Enrich (*Serving*) as Missionary Behavior

Description: Wise *embedding* means we will engage our context and participate in existing *shalom*-sowing initiatives. At times, we may start our own initiatives where we discern these could be additive to context, but our initial focus is on joining existing initiatives. We prioritize those that coincide with our own passions and spiritual convictions, as moving in ways that match our God-given gifts, interests, and personalities will give us the staying power to keep on serving for long periods of time. Local initiatives operating for the good of the city may be sourced within the church, or they may be initiatives started by people or organizations outside the church. We serve and move into various causes in the hope that missional communities might be birthed that include a rich blend of Christians and non-Christians.

In our participation in culture, we are not simply trying to be missionaries who *embed* in the subcultures of our city. We are aiming to be missionaries who pray for, provoke, and bring *shalom*. And our primary impetus in *serving* is not to rescue, save, or fix our context, but to notice and draw out whatever good we can. As we noted last chapter, we seek the Kingdom, *cultivating* the ground where God is already at work, and also creating new service opportunities where there are significant needs not being addressed. Besides demonstrating that we care, serving eventually leads to the enriching of our local context. It involves asking the kind of questions found in the learning exercise below.

Understanding Serving as a Missionary Behavior

Time: 3 to 6 hours depending upon your service project
Supplies: Whiteboard and markers, journal, pens or pencils, items appropriate to service project

1. In the gathering of the larger team, the facilitator reviews the above description of *serving* and reads aloud the sample questions below about *serving* people in your context:
    *   *What are some of my natural passions and talents that I could offer to the community?*
    *   *What are some of the ways other churches or Christian groups are serving in our city, and which ones might make sense for our team to join?*
    *   *What are some of the ways people outside the community of faith are serving locally, and which one could make sense for me and my team to join (these should be prioritized over joining other service initiatives by Christian groups)?*
    *   *How could I (my team) best serve my community, based on the intersection of my (our) interests and passions and the needs and values of the city?*
    *   *Where am I experiencing frequency or proximity with a group that is already serving in a way that interests me?*

2. Take turns sharing meaningful experiences of how you have participated in *serving* or how you have observed others practicing it well. What are some of the important contextual questions that these experiences of *serving* helped answer? Is there anything about *serving* that you don't understand?

3. Each person records in their journal the *serving* questions they feel are most relevant to the team. These questions might come from the stories shared, the list in step one, or an important idea not yet mentioned.

4. Each teammate shares with the team their top three *serving* questions. Facilitator writes them on the whiteboard.

5. Decide as a team the top three *serving* questions you would like to seek answers for in your context. Discuss initial actions you will take to answer those questions.

6. Make a simple plan for a *serving* opportunity that you can do together as a team in the next seven days.

7. Execute your plan. Meet afterwards for coffee. Evaluate your *serving* experience based on the ideals of the questions above. Journal your impressions of the experience - what you did, who responded, and how they responded.

Participating in your context in an authentic way requires also understanding yourself: the passions, abilities, gifts, and personality that you bring to your setting. The next exercise is meant to connect your own experience with what you are learning about your context.

Matching Our Collective Passions with Culture's Needs

Time: 3 to 4 hours
Supplies: Pen or pencils, sticky-notes, whiteboard and markers, SHAPE worksheet

SHAPE is an acronym developed by pastor Rick Warren, which involves:

S = Spiritual gifts
H = Heart passion
A = natural Abilities
P = Personality
E = life Experience

1. Individually: Using the following worksheet (see figure 2), take some time to fill out as many aspects of your personal "SHAPE" as you can.

2. As a team take turns sharing your individual stories. Each person gets 15 minutes without interruption. Use the grid of your SHAPE to express your story and the things that make you tick. The facilitator encourages others to ask questions at the end of each speaker's sharing time. The team takes time to suggest strengths they observe in the speaker that could help enrich their service to a wider community.

3. Reflecting on what you learned during your *absorbing* exercises, write on individual sticky-notes the needs and strengths you have observed in your context. In turn post your sticky-notes on the whiteboard. Read aloud what is written on the note as you post it.

4. Organize the sticky-notes into logical or thematic categories, and then assign a heading to each category of need or strength. Now, as a team, compare and contrast your individual SHAPEs with the needs and strengths listed. Where do you find the needs and strengths correlate with your team's SHAPEs? What needs are unmatched by the SHAPEs of your group? What strengths have a lot of connection with your SHAPEs? What SHAPEs have no present fit for the listed needs?

5. Take some time to pray for each other. What does the Holy Spirit say? Help each other identify a few ways to participate with the community in serving these needs or connecting with these strengths.

- Figure 2 –
SHAPE worksheet

CHAPTER 3

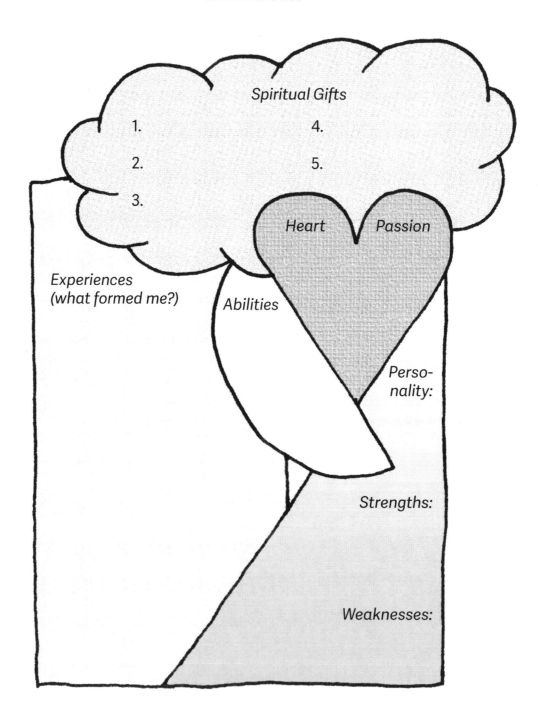

Spiritual Gifts

1. 4.

2. 5.

3.

Heart   Passion

Experiences
(what formed me?)

Abilities

Perso-
nality:

Strengths:

Weaknesses:

Debrief: *You have now had a thorough look at what it means to* **embed** *as a team in your context. You've found a way to relate to local people through neighborhood exegesis and the help of your cultural advocate. You also have an understanding of the importance of the missionary lifestyle and how the continuous pattern of three behaviors - absorbing, relating, and serving - apply to nearly every action involving the sowing of God's* **shalom***. Finally, your team has begun to match its SHAPE to the needs and strengths of your neighborhood. Remember, embedding is not merely a "startup" practice. Missionary identity and lifestyle must always remain central throughout the life of your church!*

 **MAP It!**

Turn to your Missional Action Plan in Appendix A. Go to the *Embed* section listed under *Strategy*. Review with your team the questions you find there in light of all of your work on the exercises in this chapter. Write down three embedding activities your team will commit to.

My Thoughts on *Embedding*:

What stood out the most for you in the embed *chapter?*

What questions do you still have about embed?

What was the most difficult to practice? Where were you the most deeply challenged?

Which practices seemed the most natural to you? What worked well?

What are your top three takeaways from this chapter?

Chapter 4 - Initiate: Showing and Sharing Good News (Wisely)

 It's time to respond to all we've seen and heard in our embedding. It's time to **initiate**! *Before we jump right in and make our plans, we first need to learn how to* **discern** *and* **decide** *as a team.* **Discernment** *is an extremely important practice, so we'll lead you through several personal and group exercises to help you learn it. We'll also take a deeper look at* **addressing culture**, *learning the skills to take some simple action steps to affirm what's good or help heal what's broken in our context. Finally, we'll take an in-depth look at* **evangelism** *and* **proclamation** *practices for missional teams.*

INITIATE - *establish a coordinated gospel-sowing response across an area and/or group*

By now we have spent so much time exploring, listening, and participating in the life of our part of the city that we most likely feel like it's our home. And out of the countless numbers of people we've interacted with, we've begun to see friendships growing. Some of these friends hang out with members of our team, or they join us on occasion at parties and Serve the City type events.[26] Through our friends and other relational connections we are well networked in the city. We know a great deal about this place and its rhythms, needs, joys, longings, and pain. There's so much potential for God's goodness to leave a fresh mark here!

Where do we even start? Where are those niches, those places, or those social networks that we are best suited to affect? How can we be more deliberate in sowing gospel seeds and in sharing the Good News with those we care about or with neighbors whose stories we've been privileged to hear? And how do we as a team coordinate our motions and sharing in culture, so that we actually begin to move with momentum as a missionary community?

---

26 www.servethecity.net

These are the kind of questions driving the dynamic we call *initiate*. As you see from its description above, it involves a "response" to what we've been learning through our *embedding*, our praying, and our interacting as a team. *Initiate* adds the dimensions of discernment, coordination, and facilitative leadership, as our team now tries to wisely coordinate our missionary community to follow Jesus into sustained mission and holistic evangelism.

In Gothenburg, Sweden, Marcus Fritsch and team describe the *initiate* dynamic in terms of building a counterweight or counter-balance in the culture. As Marcus puts it, any culture we encounter will have its positives, but it will also have areas where it is fallen and sick. These positives and negatives will, of course, vary from one cultural grouping to another, but in each case they become normative in their respective culture. For example, a dominant story in Western culture is that we are consumers: the "good life" is to consume material things and experiences. As a result, many westerners have become immune to the subtle and not-so-subtle manifestations of this story: greed, envy, and selfishness to name but a few. Indeed the very foundation of western economies has become consumption!

These ways of living often become so ingrained that they are difficult to see from within culture, much less to throw off. As Martin Luther once counseled, "Learn from me, how difficult a thing it is to throw off errors confirmed by the example of all the world, and which, through long habit, have become a second nature to us." We have to identify the unbalanced areas and build healthy counterweights rooted in Scripture. To

whatever degree we succeed in this, we'll likely gain more attention. *Initiating* means challenging ourselves and others to think in new ways, to help people question their worldview. As we *initiate* well, we essentially build the foundation for evangelism, for people to be ready to hear and consider the message we're proclaiming.

As teams begin to *initiate* discerned actions into context, their lifestyles and the way they treat people and God's creation will begin to stand out as life-giving and attractive. Part of the prophetic call of the body of Christ is to live in ways now that point to the Kingdom of God, while also providing a taste of that full Kingdom that's coming. As we engage culture, however, we can also be quick to identify the good that is happening there in terms of forming healthy human beings and bettering our world. Identifying the good in the world and working alongside that good can bring glory and witness to God's name as much as steering people away from damaging ways to live. To live as an alternative people, in the world but not of the world, requires both activities - visibly affirming the good coming from culture and our immediate context while at the same time resisting that which is damaging. This two-sided stance, as Marcus suggests above, helps set the stage for people to open their ears and hearts to receive God's call to life in Christ and in Christ's family.

Recognizing that culture has many positives that we can affirm, the following exercise is designed to help your team respond to the imbalances that damage people so that fresh avenues for the gospel might be opened.

Addressing Imbalances in Culture

Time: 60 to 90 minutes

Supplies: Sticky-notes, pens or pencils, whiteboard and markers

1. In small groups, name a few values that exemplify a way that culture is seducing people that are contradictory to the way of a Jesus lifestyle. Write each one on a sticky-note. Post and read them aloud to the team when prompted.

2. As a team, rank these in order of importance according to their negative impact on (or significance in) culture. The worst impact is a ten and the least a one.

3. Out of the top five, the team chooses which cultural imbalance to address. The team suggests ways to address the imbalance that are simple and could be implemented within the next 24 hours.

    Examples:
    *   For a general disrespect of public space and thus each other, one could pick up trash on their street.
    *   For a culture that is inconsiderate on the roadways, one could drive less aggressively and yield to other drivers.
    *   For a community that does not cherish its elderly, one could stop by to check up on a senior citizen, do light chores, or bring food.

4. Each individual adopts their own practice from the group suggestions and then one by one team members commit to the team what they will do to address the imbalance in culture. In one week the group will meet to tell the stories of their experiences.

Initiating Out... and Also Up and In

When we're imagining activities or practices that might correct for imbalances in culture, we are taking the posture of creating a positive counter-weight. This may involve designing a few spiritual practices that give people an alternative way to operate (e.g. practicing a sabbath rest day when our culture values 24/7 hyper-activity). But there are positive behaviors and rhythms in culture that we can build upon as well. As we noted in chapter two, we can cultivate that good ground we find in culture. In chapter five we'll take this a step further and explore how to graft our own spiritual disciplines/activities into the healthy behaviors of culture.

As part of our broader *initiating*, however, we have to get beyond simply developing our outward missional response. We need to start taking into account the deepening of our inward community as well as our spiritual formation in God. If we neglect these, our missionary activities and our proclamation will likely wear us out.

Another way to say this is to put it into the language of the elemental functions of church - Communion, Community, and Mission. These upward, inward, and outward actions result in an expression of church at its most basic level. At this *initiate* stage our team will naturally begin to strengthen not only its individual and collective capacity for mission but the other two functions as well. Our team will begin to wrestle with such questions as: How can we be a caring, supportive community to one another at this stage of our development? What can we begin to do to better promote our spiritual growth in God as individuals and as a community? As our team answers these questions and begins to *initiate* appropriate actions to address them, we are pushed to learn how to begin to operate as a small coordinated body.

One way to represent these elemental functions is with a triangle, with Mission on the leading edge. The following image captures the idea of movement into culture, rather than only a static portrayal of the three commitments. As you see, simultaneous attention is given to all three commitments, and yet we are ever on the move into culture as a people responding to our God, who is already at work before we arrive (cf. Eph. 1:22-23, where Christ is reigning over all creation - not just the church!).

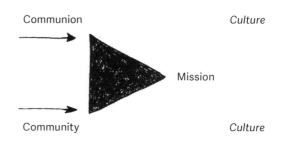

In the next chapter we'll explain how these three commitments relate to developing basic practices for discipleship. For now, we hope you find it freeing to realize that church planting begins at this most simple level. As teams discern and implement actions toward the three commitments, unique little bodies of Christ begin to emerge. And these unique little bodies are what we want to fan into flame, to grow into whatever form the Spirit and wisdom deem most suitable to our context. As the community grows, new roles and possibilities for our team grow as well, and teammates gifted in leading may begin to step up more prominently.

The communal discernment and strategic response characteristic of the *initiate* phase will ideally be continuous. From the birth of a simple missional community downstream through the development of a maturing church, teams should always be *initiating*.

As project leaders we must take pains to keep equipping and activating our people into local mission as an essential part of discipleship. This enables us to keep cultivating our context for the birth of new missional initiatives and church plants.

The Importance of Group Discernment in all Our Important Team Decisions

Because the *initiating* dynamic is about helping teams to wisely and sustainably sow the gospel into their context, it's not surprising that discernment should be of central importance. Ruth Haley Barton defines discernment as "a quality of attentiveness to God that, over time, develops into the ability to sense God's heart and purpose in any given moment."[27] Discernment practices help the team base their decision-making and gospel-sowing on wisdom and the Spirit's leading, and not simply on good ideas.

If we polled most church planting teams, we might be surprised to find how few actually know anything at all about communal discernment. Decision-making is often based on a set of practical considerations, superficial leadings, and at times only on the lone team leader's sense of "hearing from the Lord." In Communitas we strongly encourage teams to define a good discernment process for their key decision-making, as they will need to continually employ that process over the life of their project. But how does a team define such a process? Let's delve into that a bit.

As Elijah discovered, God's voice often does not come in thunder or earthquakes, but comes small and sweet. The only way that we can hear that voice is to slow down, calm down, and listen. Listening requires space, time, and often discipline. Listening is hard enough to do as individuals when we try to hear God's voice. It becomes even more difficult as a team attempting to discern God's voice together.

The first principle of discerning God's voice as a team is to be discerning as individuals. Each person on the team needs to practice recognizing the difference between their own will and God's will, learning to answer the question "Do I truly desire God's will more than anything else?" Or as Ignatian spirituality puts it: "Am I indifferent to anything but the will of God?" As individuals in the group increase their own capacity to discern God's will, they will be better able to bring this into group decision-making.

Discerning together is not easy work. It requires a depth of relying on each other that brings out primal instincts of self-protection, patterns of distrust inherited from our families or other communities, and our own false-selves. And even once discernment is experienced, it is not maintained randomly or haphazardly.

In order to do this hard work together, strong commitment is needed. The core of this commitment is to Christ and His call on our lives. In response to this primary call, our team then commits to clear values that define the safe space for listening, practices that bring those values to life, and a covenant that puts this commitment into words. If your team has not yet identified its core values, there is a helpful exercise for that in Appendix I.

Acts 15 provides an amazing example of God's people discerning His will, His longing, together. Whatever question your team might be facing, it is probably

---

27 Ruth Haley Barton, *Pursuing God's Will Together: A Discernment Practice for Leadership Groups* (Downers Grove: InterVarsity Press, 2012), 57.

nothing compared to what this decision-making body had to face. Because of Paul's work among non-Jewish people, large numbers were following Jesus as their Lord. But Jesus and His followers up until this point were still Jewish, their leaders were Jewish, and they were meeting in synagogues and even the temple. The core covenant symbol of their relationship to God was circumcision. Many in the young church argued that these new followers needed to be circumcised - essentially that new believers needed to become Jewish - as evidence of their commitment to worship Jesus. Paul and others disagreed. Acts 15 tells the story of how the leaders discerned God's longing for His young church on this core identity issue. Their discernment enabled them to wisely address a major conflict.

As disagreements so commonly flare up among teams, we provide the following exercise to help your team develop a healthy discernment practice for resolving conflict.

Developing a Group Discernment Practice for Resolving Conflict

Time: 60 minutes
Supplies: Bible, journal, pens or pencils

1. Read Acts 15 through five times before coming to this discussion. Note in your journal what jumps out at you from the passage. This could be repeated words, repeated themes, or unusual concepts.

2. In small groups make note of the key conflicts that the Jerusalem Council were considering. Respond to the following prompts:
    *   *What did they discern to be their core issues?*
    *   *What was at stake? Which issues seem to come up the most?*
    *   *What did they decide to do and why?*
    *   *Which values seemed to be most important to them given the level of conflict?*

3. Study the examples below. These are rules written by other faith communities to determine what to do when faced with conflict. What do you notice about these examples?

    Example: *Before we make a decision as to what to do, our team will ask the question, "Who will be left out by our decision?"*

    Example: *When engaging in a conflict, our team will hear all sides of the story before making a decision. We will call in a third party if necessary for objectivity.*

4. Read the following passage aloud in your groups.

The Jerusalem Council was struggling with a few issues. One was what to do with Paul's practice as a missionary in light of the accusations of the Judaizers. Did they have a point or not? Peter and James had already given Paul the go ahead quite a few years earlier. Paul wanted to know if they still stood with him. The Council summarized that unity was the most important issue, whereas the Judaizers argued for adherence to the Mosaic Law. The Council made their decision based on a value of unity that would allow the Jews and non-Jews to enjoy table fellowship - a huge step considering the law-abiding Jews thought the non-Jews were repulsive barbarians. In the end a wise way forward was discerned, and unity prevailed. What will your team do when faced with such deep-seated conflict?

5. Imagine what you would have done if you were Peter and James. With your small group and with the examples above in mind, write a rule that you think the Jerusalem Council would have written, given their decision. Share your rule with the team when the facilitator prompts you.

6. How will you incorporate unity into your values? What rule would you write for yourself? Take five minutes individually and write your own rule. Share with the team when prompted.

The first part of a practice of communal discernment is properly setting the stage. As a start we'll want to make sure that the right people are present and part of the process. Include people responsible for making the decision and for carrying out the decision, but also include people who are affected by the outcome of the decision. The next action to set the stage is to ask the right question. A question as simple as "which night should we meet?" might actually disguise the deeper question of "what kind of people do we want to feel welcome among us?" In other words, not all questions require a full discernment process, but some questions will become more profound when we come to realize what is really being asked. One other way we prepare our hearts for discernment is by reaffirming the core values of the group along with the broader story that brought us to this place. When we have a crisp, important question in view, and when we have reminded ourselves about our values and story, we are ready to move deeper into the discernment process.

The next aspect of communal discernment involves inner work - placing ourselves humbly before God to ask: "Am I truly open to Your will for us?" We need to take time to examine our hearts for pride, mistrust, personal agendas, or dreams. Anything that might stand in the way of hearing God's true longing must be surrendered. We ask ourselves, "What needs to die in me in order for the will of God to find room in my life?" We allow the Holy Spirit to convict us and prepare us. After a time of examining ourselves in the light of such questions, both individually and as a group, we acknowledge our full dependence on the wisdom of God and our complete trust in Him.

Finally, we are ready to listen to the options, the issues, the plans, the possibilities. We listen to the back-story that has brought us to this point. We listen to each other and the impressions and the concerns we have. We access the facts, the Word, and everything we have learned in our *embedding* process that may have relevance to our central question. We tune into outside voices and inside experiences. We brainstorm, dialogue, discuss, and try to make each and every viable option the best it could possibly be. The intensity and time we give to this listening and weighing of inputs will vary according to the complexity and potential impact of our discernment question. During all this hard work together, we continue to be attentive to the voice of God, who often provides both clear insights and also subtle nudges.

When we have reached a point where we can identify one or more possible courses of action, we break for silence. This pause gives place to the Holy Spirit to add further insight, guidance, and comfort. In very complex decisions that will likely have notable impact (e.g. people, finances, ministry opportunities/limitations, etc.), it may be wise to give a day or more to reflect on the possibilities we've identified.

Our time of discernment ends when we agree together on a decision. Agreement can take a variety of forms, from whole-hearted consensus to a tentative willingness to move forward. In most situations, the communal will needed to stay the course or continue on mission together cannot be upheld by a majority-rule vote or point leader veto. Each community will need to decide what agreement and disagreement means for them. The Quakers offer a form of consensus that ranges from "I agree without reservation" through "I do not agree for these reasons but am willing to defer" to "I cannot move forward with this decision." Each team will also need to factor in whether a given decision is reversible or not. With some choices, we as a leadership team can back pedal or change course if the outworking of a decision proves to weaken or harm the community. With other choices, there's "no going back" or no easy way to undo what's been done. If a looming decision must be made that cannot be reversed, our discernment process will likely require greater time, sensitivity, and consensus.

After all this work of listening, processing, and deciding, we come to rest again. We silence our souls and create space to hear God's affirmation and/or any further Word.

But discernment doesn't end with a decision; discernment ends with action. We have examined what we know and what has been revealed to us by God, and it's time to steward this knowledge. God gifts us with such decision making so that we might act on the light that is given. This is what God holds us accountable to.

One very important principle to always keep in mind through the entire process of making important decisions as a team: it's not so much about making the *right decision* together, but doing the best we can in light of God's love and leading to make a *good decision*. In Appendices F, G, and H we have provided a sampling of spiritual practices that may aid your group discernment process (Lectio Divina, Ignatian Examen, Movements in Corporate Leadership Discernment). Our included sample is by no means exhaustive, and we encourage you to seek out others you may find more suitable. The following exercise is designed to guide you in employing a spiritual practice for the purpose of group discernment.

Spiritual Practices for Discernment

Time: 2 to 4 hours
Supplies: Journal, pens or pencils, Appendix F, G or H

1. In small groups, go back to the **Addressing Imbalances in Culture** exercise earlier in this chapter. Choose a problem that culture is urging people into that is most foreboding when attempting to embody the Jesus lifestyle. It should be an imbalance other than the one you have already acted upon.

2. Go to the Appendix and choose a Spiritual Discernment Practice.

3. Sit prayerfully with your small group and go through the practice together with the problem from step one in mind.

4. When you are finished, respond to these questions:
   - *What approach will your team take to address the problem?*
   - *Which values will you exemplify? How will you exemplify them?*
   - *What one action will you take as a group to address your problem?*

5. Gather as a team and tell about the pros and cons of your discernment process. What was helpful, what was not? Where does the work lie for you in this discernment process? Continue as a team to identify practices that keep you open to hearing God's will.

6. Take a few moments to journal your reflections on this exercise.

So, discernment is the starting point for determining how we as a team ought to proceed forward. In a great field of missional opportunities, being able to wisely choose what to say "yes" to and what to say "no" to can be the key to survival. *Initiating* enables our group to demonstrate and proclaim the gospel in a much more targeted and enduring sense. It's a combination of healthy decision-making and robust forward motion.

Proclaiming Good News as We Relate and Serve in Christ's Name

A vital part of *initiating* is helping people find their way to faith in Christ. Teams need to put serious prayer into this effort. Often people today in Western cultures come to faith in Christ only after an extended period of belonging to Christian community in some form. Whereas in past generations many came to belief by being convinced of the logic or rational appeal of the Christian message, people now commonly need to experience authentic Christ-community before faith makes sense to them. They no longer simply believe certain things and thereby officially belong to the church; people now commonly need to *belong before they believe*. It's the up-close experience of both Jesus-loving people and also a transformational way of life that helps them "see the light" and believe.

Church historian Stuart Murray notes that when Christianity became more mainstream in the 4th century, it became easier for people to consider themselves part of the faith simply because they belonged to a church and believed the right things. Eventually, this allowed moral laxity to creep into the church, as the emphasis shifted away from adopting a way of life that demanded obedience to Christ. Christianity became more about confessing creeds and engaging in church rituals than about behaving or acting like Jesus within the vibrancy of a living relationship with God. In similar fashion today, the gospel has been somewhat masked by "church-ianity" where the focus is on believing right doctrines and going to church to perform religious duties. To actually see the truth and make the choice to follow Jesus, more and more people now need this whole package of *belonging* in Christian community as well as *behaving* in Christ-like ways.[28]

As a group *embeds* and first begins to *initiate* a coordinated gospel-sowing response in its context, it is a good time to intentionally find ways to include and involve those who are not yet Christians. This might mean creating relational spheres for belonging, such as special interest groups, weekly interaction times at a local pub, faith-processing groups like the Alpha Course, or compassion initiatives such as Serve the City. These lines of service and relational belonging provide natural spheres for us to exchange our stories and, as the Spirit leads, proclaim Jesus and God's good news.

Finding ways to invite people into belonging and participating while they explore faith is only one side of the coin. Too often the measures taken by a core group to include and involve non-Christians are only of the invitational, "come to us" variety. Such measures need to be complemented by ones that involve us "going to them." A team needs to be asking, "What might we be invited to by those outside our ranks? Who is extending us an invitation to belong and participate, and what is already operating that we might join?" We would do well to learn from Jesus, who seemed to look for opportunities to be invited in (and in the case of Zaccheaus in Luke 19:1-10, Jesus actually went a step further and invited Himself to be a guest in Zacchaeus' home!).

Whatever a team chooses to do to include and involve outsiders, their serving and relating ought to be a good match with the team's energy, capacity, and collective discernment. This stewarding of the team's inner reserves, giftedness, passions, and leadings helps insure sustainability, while also protecting them from burnout and being spread too thin.

The next exercise will help your team explore two aspects of belonging and behaving: offering it to those who need it, and accessing it in spaces that already exist in your city.

---

28 Stuart Murray, *Post-Chrisendom: Church and Mission in a Strange New World* (Waynesboro: Paternoster, 2005), 64-73.

Cultivating Opportunities for Belonging and Behaving

Time: 2 hours
Supplies: Whiteboard and markers

This learning exercise consists of two parts to help you cultivate the two aspects of *belonging* and *behaving* opportunities: Offering and Accessing.

Before beginning the exercises, review the following definitions with your team:

Belonging *opportunities are repeatable occasions to include our friends in events, activities, or common interest groups that also involve others from our team or faith community. Examples include sports teams, book clubs, poker nights, and neighborhood activities.*

Behaving *opportunities are occasions that allow not-yet-Christians to participate in discipling practices toward the goal of spiritual formation. These opportunities might occur within our faith community or in partnership with another group. Examples include: Bible study/reflection groups, creative worship experiences, group prayer times, or regular service (shalom-sowing) projects.*

Part 1: Offering Opportunities for Belonging and Behaving

1. Gathered as a team name a few not-yet-Christian folks who are on the margins of your group. The facilitator writes their names on the whiteboard. Those who know him or her give a brief description of each person.

2. Considering the interests and personality of the individual names on the board:
   - Suggest as many ways as you can to offer *belonging* opportunities to each person on the board.
   - Suggest as many ways as you can to provide *behaving* opportunities to each person on the board.

3. Discuss the following with your team: Taking into account the gifts, interests, and leadings of your team, who would be the best at inviting each person into one or more of the belonging or behaving opportunities you've listed? How would they offer the invitation?

Part 2: Accessing Opportunities for Belonging and Behaving

1. Name the good causes, clubs, interest groups, recreational sports leagues, etc. in your city that are of interest to your team. While these may not be formative in a "Christian discipleship" sense, they often can foster relational connection and openness to God/spirituality. Facilitator writes these on the board. Respond to the following prompts:
    *   *What interests you about these groups?*
    *   *How could individuals from your team (or perhaps the whole team) become involved in the networks, groups, and social service initiatives of non-Christians in your area?*
    *   *How would involvement with these groups provide greater access to belonging and behaving opportunities to the people you identified above? How might such involvement be a bridge to the belonging and behaving opportunities offered by your faith community?*

2. Pairs from the team volunteer to visit one or more of these groups in the coming week.

3. At your next team gathering, tell the story of your visits and assess together the experience. What steps will you take this week to invite others to join you in participating in one or more of these opportunities?

Initiating is not only about what we do. It is also about what we say. In speaking about proclamation - what we typically label evangelism - we often miss a couple of important things. In the first place, evangelism is about proclaiming good news. In the New Testament, the word we translate as *gospel* actually means *good news*. The Latin version of this same Greek word, *evangel*, forms the basis of the English verb "to evangelize." Though it would not be proper grammar to say it this way, when we evangelize a friend, we are essentially *good-newsing* him or her. To be an evangelist is to be a bringer of good tidings. It is perhaps helpful to remember this as we speak of Jesus to those not knowing Him. Does good news mark both our manner and our message? Do we so focus on the bad news of human sin and separation from God that it muffles our good news? Do we treat people as our projects rather than with the same dignity and enduring love that Jesus offered? We share good news, and through our caring we *are* good news to people.

Another thing often missing when talking about evangelism is the simplicity of what we are proclaiming - a living Person. I, Dan, once asked a group of Christian friends what we mean when we use the word, gospel. What is this good news we are proclaiming? Some said the Kingdom of God is near - God's good rule over all creation is freshly displayed in the coming of God's Son. Some mentioned that Christ died on a cross for the sins of the world that we might be forgiven and adopted as God's children. Others said that the good news is that Jesus the Messiah reigns, not any modern day Caesar, nor any other power. Still others mentioned that God is reconciling and making all things new – setting humans in right relationship to God, people in right relationship to each other, and setting free all creation from corruption, decay, and death.

All of these definitions are arguably part of the good news, and there's even more to add. But what

I noticed was missing in all our church-world definitions was Jesus Christ the living Person. When we bring good news, we announce the coming of the risen, living One. Whatever words we choose to describe the gospel, we are bearing witness to a very alive, loving God. The Story in which Jesus is situated is vastly important and is part of the layers of the gospel we share. But it is this Jesus we know and love and relate to that is the essence of our good news, and only secondarily the gospel as concepts to understand or as a captivating storyline we can tell to others. As 1 John 1:1 puts it, "That which was from the beginning, which we have heard, which we have seen with our eyes, which we have looked at and our hands have touched--this we proclaim concerning the Word of life." We proclaim the message and we proclaim the living Person of Jesus Christ.

As teams *initiate* activities to demonstrate and proclaim the gospel, it is good to rally around a common definition of what it means to engage in evangelism. Though there are many ways people define this, one author of a popular book on evangelism defined the term this way:

Evangelism is that set of loving, intentional activities governed by the goal of initiating persons into Christian discipleship in response to the reign of God.[29]

The following series of exercises is designed to help you discern and develop an approach to evangelism that's appropriate for your context.

---

29 Scott J. Jones, *The Evangelistic Love of God and Neighbor: A Theology of Witness and Discipleship* (Nashville: Abingdon Press, 2003), 18.

Creating Your Own Definition of Evangelism and Discerning its Practice

Time: 60 to 90 minutes
Supplies: Journal, pens or pencils, whiteboard and markers, sticky-notes

This exercise is broken up into two parts: personal reflection and group reflection.

Personal reflection:

1. Write out the definition above of evangelism. Leave lots of space between each word and each line. Then, respond to the prompts below:
    *   *What do you find that you like in this definition? Circle those parts/words.*
    *   *What would you say is missing, unclear, or poorly worded? Cross out those phrases/words.*
    *   *What needs to be added? Add in those thoughts/words where appropriate.*
    *   *You may want to add something about Holy Spirit guidance.*
    *   *Scriptural references may be important to you; add them as you're led to.*
    *   *You may add something that is specific to the people group that you work with.*

2. When you are done with your surgery on this definition, write out your own cohesive definition of evangelism in your journal and on a sticky-note.

Team reflection:

1. Take turns sharing your evangelism definitions. Post your notes on the whiteboard and read them aloud to the team. Listen attentively to the definitions of others.

2. After everyone has shared their definition, the group compiles a list of intended outcomes of your evangelism. Facilitator will write these on the whiteboard. Under each outcome, list two or three actions that would inspire these outcomes.

    Examples:

Outcome:	Person learns God is trustworthy
Actions:	Tell of a time when God proved trustworthy in my life.
	Model trustworthiness to them.
Outcome:	Person learns they can talk to God
Actions:	Ask them if they have ever prayed before.
	Offer to pray for them (model prayer for them).

3. As you survey the list of intended outcomes, respond to these discussion prompts by suggesting a few action items for the hinder/help scenarios.

Hinder:
- *What are you up against in your context that will hinder these aims?*
- *Discuss ways you might reduce or lower the effect of those things that seem to stand in the way of effective evangelism in your context.*

Help:
- *What does the culture offer that will help you in your particular context?*
- *How will you leverage those positive aspects of your context?*

4. As your facilitator records these on the whiteboard, add them to your journal. Choose one action item to practice with a partner this week.

5. The team meets in one week. Report your results back to the larger team, evaluating your own success or failure to accomplish the outcomes. Do your outcomes need revising? If so, the team sets a time to adjust them.

CHAPTER 4

Now that we've arrived at a working definition of evangelism and set of outcomes we hope for, let's take a look at how Jesus and Paul evangelized. Surely there's a lot we can learn from their approach!

Let's first consider Jesus' "good-newsing."

Comparing Jesus' Good-Newsing to our Own

Time: 60 to 90 minutes
Supplies: Bible or copies of John 4, journal, pens or pencils

1. In small groups, take turns reading John 4:1-38 three times out loud. What stands out to you?

2. Analyze the progression of Jesus' encounter with the Samaritan woman. In your journal write down His strategy as bullet points. Next to each bullet point note the value that Jesus exemplifies.

3. Take turns telling of a time when you good-newsed someone. If you have never done this, tell of a time when you witnessed someone else doing it, or when someone good-newsed you.

4. After each story is told, respond to these prompts:
   - *Name the values that were embraced.*
   - *Given Jesus' example, how could it have been different, and maybe more effective?*
   - *What have you heard from each other that might encourage you in your own evangelism?*

Of course, Jesus is God, so maybe it's a little unfair to draw too much from His way of evangelizing. But we can at least acknowledge that the ways in which He operates are worth trying to imitate: Jesus engaged in social conversation, moving His conversation about spiritual things into the public sphere. In the John 4 passage cited in the exercise above, Jesus used the immediate example of the water she was drawing as a way to talk about deeper issues and to stimulate spiritual interest. Jesus, though knowing the woman's sordid history, did not condemn her. He also stuck to the core issue at hand, refusing to be distracted by the woman's attempts to dodge His questions. Instead, Jesus guided the conversation back toward what was most important and called her to respond to the reality that this was the Messiah standing right before her. It is especially important to note Christ's attitude of humility throughout the encounter. Humility should characterize every aspect of our evangelism. As well, note Christ's willingness to boldly cross cultural boundaries in the name of bringing living water to people, especially those too easily missed or looked down upon, as, in this case, a Samaritan woman.

Now let's consider the Apostle Paul's approach to evangelism.

Observing and Applying Principles from Paul's Evangelism

Time: 60 to 90 minutes
Supplies: Bible, journal, pen or pencil

1. Read II Cor. 5:17-21 through a few times, at least once aloud. Then respond to these prompts in your journal:
   - *What drove Paul to share the gospel so fearlessly?*
   - *What was at the heart of Paul's message of good news?*
   - *What did he seem to care about the most? (HINT: What was repeated?)*

2. Read Acts 16. Respond to these prompts in your journal:
   - *When and how did Paul rely on God?*
   - *Where do you see evidence of Paul's strategic planning?*
   - *How does a demonstration of God's power open up doors for the gospel?*

3. Read Titus chapters 2 and 3 carefully. Respond to these prompts in your journal:
   - *The word "tact" is defined as: 1) a keen sense of what to say or do to avoid giving offense; 2) skill in dealing with difficult or delicate situations. Although Paul does not use the word tact, he urges various groups of Christ followers to act in this manner. Identify instances where he asks his readers to exercise tact for the sake of the gospel. What else do you notice in Paul's strategy?*
   - *What do you suppose was Paul's greatest reason for asking the Cretan Christians to be tactful in their behavior? How might this apply to your practice of evangelism?*

As with Jesus, it is a bit unfair to us to try to draw too much from these Bible passages to inform our present day evangelism. After all, none of us are Apostles today in the way Paul was to the early church. However, we do see elements that are applicable to us. In his exhortation to the Corinthians (II Cor. 5:17-21), Paul's evangelism involved a passionate sense of urgency. He did not simply proclaim but he held a heartfelt, crisp sense of how important it was for people not to tarry but to receive God's gift and be reconciled. He uses the word "reconciled" in various forms five times in this short passage, as he so desired that people respond and close that gap between themselves and God.

In the Acts 16 storyline, we see Paul turning to both common sense and reliance on God's power and leading in evangelism. We see him wisely choosing to circumcise Timothy to enhance the hearing of the gospel among the Jews. The writer Luke then shows Paul moving in his call to the gentiles but ever sensitive to God's leading and timing. God blocks their progress in Bithynia for the moment and directs them to the region of Macedonia. There, Paul makes a strategic decision to skip doing ministry in the city of Neopolis in order to get to Philippi, the leading city of the district. In Philippi they settle "for several days," and find out about a place of prayer where seekers gathered, and then inhabit that as a hotspot for sharing Christ. Paul and team keep moving forward as God opens doors. Lydia is converted, and she hosts Paul's growing group. The gospel's progress all along is enhanced through God's validating the good news with power. Certainly we can imitate Paul's attention to good planning, his reliance on God's moment-by-moment leading, and his expectancy for God to move at times in power.

Finally, in chapters two and three of Titus, we see over and over again Paul's dedication to helping his Christian sisters and brothers behave in ways that are advantageous to the gospel. In their households, in their vocations, in their participation as good citizens in society - in whatever roles they find themselves in - they ought to behave with tact so that their reputation and lifestyle make the gospel more attractive (cf. Titus 2:4-5; 2:8; 2:9-10; 3:1-2; 3:14). And lest we get in trouble citing Paul's counsel to women and slaves here, let us be clear about what he seems to be teaching. Paul was not condoning slavery, or in the case of women, insisting that they remain "busy at home," as if these instructions were the unchanging will of God (2:5). Paul asks for this patient endurance of hardship by slaves and women because in this cultural context both slavery and vocationally confining women to the home front were societal norms. Paul's immediate goal was not to overthrow the old order. It seems he believed that the principles of the gospel would eventually iron out these imbalances over time. The goal at present was to give people no reason to "malign the word of God," and also to "in every way make the teaching about God our Savior attractive."

All this to say, whether following Christ's or Paul's example, our church communities and any group wearing the name "Christian" ought to live together responsibly, humbly, and attractively to the host culture, so that people might be drawn to explore the message and Person behind those attitudes and actions - Jesus.

Many people are shy or reluctant to talk about big issues like the topics addressed in the Gospel. Therefore, a shrewd missionary seeks comfortable ways to build friendships with people. These provide avenues of access to a culture with fewer barriers, and they express hospitality to a culture in bite-size portions. They involve relating to people beyond small talk. Easy avenues of access to people might involve the common ground of local music, dance, foods, a specific kind of gift giving, festivals, art, recreational activities, etc. The story below from Deborah Loyd illustrates an example of discovering an easy avenue of access.

We planned to start a church in a politically and socially liberal metropolitan area of Portland. We knew the people attracted to our project were the young hipster crowd (our heart burst). We did not have any problem making friends and having conversations over coffee. They were intrigued with us for a few reasons, but as the weeks drew on it became clear that they would not make any commitments to a church community even though they thirsted for a spiritual practice that would make sense to them. Although they kept coffee dates with us and we had many stimulating spiritual conversations, there was no further commitment. We were perplexed as to what to do next. How could we offer hospitality that spoke their language?

And then our 18 year old daughter said, "Make it look like a club, dark and loud. Supply the instruments and let them design the building." After discovering the de-facto leader of the community, we made a proposal to him because we observed that others trusted him and followed his lead. He could invite anyone he wanted to the project of building a space for his community. We would supply the budget and they would guide how the building was decorated, which instruments would be included, and what the social priorities would be. He trusted us for the spiritual priorities. Together we would create the community. On our first day we had 82 musicians, artists, and dancers show up, and for eleven years attendance never dipped lower than that. As it turned out, our young daughter knew more about approaching the community than we did. She was our prophet. What were

the avenues to accessing the culture? Music, art, dance, and empowering the leader of the community, but most of all creative control.

A few years later we ended up in a similar situation with a group of young people who live outdoors. We wanted them to feel welcome in our community of faith. Where did we discover access? In peanut butter and jelly sandwiches, coffee, and cigarettes. Many churches give out food but not many churches are comfortable giving out cigarettes. I certainly was not. In spite of my protestations, the community proceeded, and the community was right. Our friends who live outdoors began coming to our weekly meetings. They began volunteering with clean up and eventually some joined the worship team. How did our community discover this access point? They went downtown where our friends gathered, observed them, and noted what their community valued most. Then they tested their hypothesis and confirmed their observations. Thus the cigarette outreach was launched. Since then two more churches have been birthed which serve over four hundred disenfranchised folks in our city.... and hand out cigarettes.

While distributing cigarettes to marginalized people in our city may seem rather unconventional in some circles, Deborah's story illustrates that sometimes, unconventional means are precisely what is needed to gain inroads into another culture. All cultures have these avenues of access. The difficulty for us as outsiders is to find them. The following exercise will help your team discover your own, potentially surprising, avenues of access to culture.

Discovering Avenues of Access to the Culture

Time: 60 minutes

Supplies: Access to the Internet, journals, pens or pencils

1. In small groups, review your notes on II Cor. 5, Acts 16 and Titus 2-3 from the Learning Exercise **Observing and Applying Principles from Paul's Evangelism** earlier in this chapter. Review the way Paul engaged in evangelism, and also the way he encouraged the early church to conduct itself according to the values of that specific culture. What values was Paul speaking to? List them in your journals.

2. Now consider your own specific context or the culture that you wish to reach. Here are a few questions to consider that are reflective of cultural values:
    *   *Are they matriarchal or patriarchal?*
    *   *How do they treat those who are weaker?*
    *   *What is the value of work in their culture?*
    *   *What about resources or ownership of land?*
    *   *How do they give and receive gifts?*
    *   *What marks belonging?*
    *   *What religious practices do you notice?*
    *   *How long does it take for an outsider to belong?*
    *   *What part does art or beauty play in their cultural understandings?*
    *   *How do they use language?*
    *   *What does their society revolve around?*
    *   *What do they value most?*
    *   *Whatever else you might be curious about that would give you an avenue of entrance into the culture.*

3. Each person in your small group will choose one of the above questions to respond to. Then, they will go online or talk to their cultural advocate to research contextual information for the chosen question. What do your findings tell you about the values of your context?

4. Report your findings to your small group. Develop a few strategies of approach for your context according to what you have researched.

5. Choose one avenue of access and make a plan to practice it with your small group within the month. Schedule a meeting time with the team to meet and share your experiences.

Accenting the Communal Side of Evangelism

We started this chapter discussing the need for discernment to be a communal behavior. That collective discernment allows members of the team to wisely define both their individual and communal commitment to sharing the gospel. While it's important for every member of a team and community to do their part in evangelism (and we will touch on this individual role briefly), we want to spend most of the rest of this chapter emphasizing the collective role of the local body of Christ in evangelism while also showing how those uniquely gifted for evangelism fit in the picture.

Author and evangelist Michael Frost claims that every follower of Christ is called to live in such a way that it inspires non-Christian people to ask questions about God, faith, and our way of life. However, Frost argues that saying every believer is an evangelist is a myth; instead, he says the Apostle Paul assumes a twofold approach when it comes to evangelism. Paul, writing as both an apostle and as a gifted evangelist, writes the church in Colossae:

[2] "Devote yourselves to prayer, being watchful and thankful. [3] And pray for us, too, that God may open a door for our message, so that we may proclaim the mystery of Christ, for which I am in chains. [4] Pray that I may proclaim it clearly, as I should. [5] Be wise in the way you act toward outsiders; make the most of every opportunity. [6] Let your conversation be always full of grace, seasoned with salt, so that you may know how to answer everyone." – Col. 4:2-6

Paul asks the Colossians to pray for evangelists, for both opportunities to share Christ and for courage to proclaim the gospel. But he doesn't emphasize the Colossians praying for themselves as much as simply asking them to pray for the evangelists' ministry. The role of average believers who are not evangelistically-gifted (as per Eph. 4:11) is to wisely conduct themselves toward outsiders and to look for opportunities to answer the questions posed.

Essentially, Frost argues that evangelists are to proclaim and believers are to give answers. He captures this distinction in this useful table:

Paul's Twofold Approach to Evangelism in the Church

Type of Minister	Priorities	Type of Spoken Ministry
Gifted Evangelists	Clarity in the gospel; looking for opportunities	Bold proclamation
Evangelistic Believers	Prayer; watchfulness; wise socializing	Gracious answers

Frost claims the Apostle Peter is in agreement with Paul. Consider I Peter 3:15-16, for instance:

[15] "But in your hearts revere Christ as Lord. Always be prepared to give an answer to everyone who asks you to give the reason for the hope that you have. But do this with gentleness and respect, [16] keeping a clear conscience, so that those who speak maliciously against your good behavior in Christ may be ashamed of their slander."[30]

---

30 Michael Frost, *Surprise the World: The Five Habits of Highly Missional People* (Colorado Springs: Navpress, 2016), 1-7 (Table used by permission).

Whether or not this two-fold distinction is adequate to describe the difference between the ministries of gifted evangelists and evangelistic believers, it does help us to see that both the more rare "big E" evangelists and the typical "little e" evangelists must work together. As they work together, the team or church becomes more effective in evangelism. Frost's ideas emphasize that a church's simple, united display of the Jesus life leads people to ask questions.[31]

This communal display of an attractive gospel life is certainly a strong theme in the New Testament. Consider when Jesus says in Matthew 5:13-16:

[13] "You are the salt of the earth. But if the salt loses its saltiness, how can it be made salty again? It is no longer good for anything, except to be thrown out and trampled underfoot. [14] You are the light of the world. A town built on a hill cannot be hidden. [15] Neither do people light a lamp and put it under a bowl. Instead they put it on its stand, and it gives light to everyone in the house. [16] In the same way, let your light shine before others, that they may see your good deeds and glorify your Father in heaven."

Unlike our frequent individualistic reading of these verses, the Lord is speaking to His people corporately.

We also see this communal role in proclamation taught all throughout Paul's letter to Titus. And Philippians 2:14-16 (The Message) perhaps captures Paul's teaching best:

"Do everything readily and cheerfully—no bickering, no second-guessing allowed! Go out into the world uncorrupted, a breath of fresh air in this squalid and polluted society. Provide people with a glimpse of good living and of the living God. Carry the light-giving Message into the night so I'll have good cause to be proud of you on the day that Christ returns. You'll be living proof that I didn't go to all this work for nothing."

As author Bryan Stone once put it,

"Christian evangelism is fundamentally rooted in ecclesiology. It can even be said the church does not need an evangelistic strategy. The church is the evangelistic strategy."[32]

The following exercise will help your team deepen their understanding of the role of community in evangelism as well as create a plan to put this into action.

---

31   Interestingly, Frost presents an example of a church living the sort of "questionable life" that he is talking about. Small Boat Big Sea, in Sydney, Australia, has defined a rhythm of spiritual life that is captured by five simple practices. That rhythm, which we describe in greater detail on page 91, goes by the acronym, B.E.L.L.S.: Bless, Eat, Listen to the Spirit, Learn Christ and His ways, act as Sent ones (looking for opportunities to alert people to the reign of God). After more than a decade of living this way, it is safe to say that this way of life continues to provoke many questions by those outside church!

---

32   Bryan P. Stone, *Evangelism after Christendom: The Theology and Practice of Christian Witness* (Grand Rapids: Brazos, 2006),15.

The Community's Role in Evangelism

Time: 60 minutes

Supplies: Whiteboard and markers, journal, pens and pencils

1. Silently read the following quotes. Underline the words or concepts that you find interesting or important.

   The Church must indwell the Christian story. It is the indwelling and embodiment of the Christian story that makes it comprehensible (and perhaps even appealing) to society. It is the actions of the Christian community that exegete the Christian message. To say that Christians believe in God is 'true but uninteresting' until the community takes a certain shape to reveal the character of the Christian God.[33] - Daniel Oudshoorn

   The congregation must be so deeply and intimately involved in the secular concerns of the neighborhood that it becomes clear to everyone that no one or nothing is outside the range of God's love in Jesus... It must be clear that the local congregation cares for the well-being of the whole community and not just for itself... But, and this reminder is very necessary, this involvement must not become something that muffles the distinctive note of the gospel. The church ought not to fit so comfortably into the situation that it is simply welcomed as one of the well-meaning agencies of philanthropy.[34] - Lesslie Newbigin

2. In small groups, take turns telling what you underlined. Why was it significant to you? What inspires you?

3. Still in small groups, take turns responding to these prompts:
   - *How might your team and community take "shape to reveal the character of the Christian God?" in ways that also preserve "the distinctive note of the gospel?"*
   - *If it is "the actions of the Christian community that exegete [or translate] the Christian message," what specific behaviors could you adopt that would help people know that you both love God and also care about "the well-being of the whole community?"*

4. Gathered as a team, each small group shares its responses to the above questions. Facilitator writes these on the whiteboard.

---

33 Daniel Oudshoorn, *"Speaking Christianly as a Missional Activity in the Midst of Babel"* (Stimulus, Vol. 14, No 1, February 2006).

34 Paul Weston, *Lesslie Newbigin: Missionary Theologian: A Reader* (Grand Rapids: Wm. B. Eerdmans, 2006), 145.

Dynamic Adventure

5. Together as a team, decide on:
   - One way that you as a team or faith community might shape yourselves to better reveal the character of God.
   - Two ways you might consistently act as a community that both demonstrate the gospel and show that you care about the well-being of your neighborhood or city.

6. As a team, develop a simple plan you can utilize as a community practice to help you act on your decisions in step 5. In the previous exercise **Discovering Avenues of Access to the Culture** you practiced new avenues of access to the context. Name a few approaches that were successful. How could you build on those as a community to better "reveal the character of God" and "demonstrate the gospel in your neighborhood?" Note these in your journal and discuss them as you develop your plan.

7. Set a date with your team to begin your new community practice. Set another date for follow up evaluation.

8. Implement your plan and then debrief according to your schedule!

Other Strategies to Help Us Become Better Evangelizers

Missional communities need to live well, in the power of the Spirit, to provoke questions from outsiders that might lead to opportunities to share the good news. But what other strategies might be helpful to mobilize the body into proclamation? Here are a few you might consider, and we invite you to come up with your own list.

- Evangelist and founder of Communitas, Linus Morris, when asked about the single most effective way to move communities into evangelism, had this to offer: "Ask questions, express genuine interest in people's lives. Eventually, over time, you will find the conversations grow so weighted on your neighbor's side that they will finally start asking you questions about your life." How are we as listeners who come armed with questions and patience?

- How many of us have seen people come to faith because word/life are united with Holy Spirit power displays? In Acts 13, Paul encounters a Jewish sorcerer, Simon Bar Jesus, and pronounces blindness upon him in judgment for the man's attempt to block the gospel's progress. The text tells us the proconsul (senator),"an intelligent man," believes when he sees what had happened, "for he was amazed at the teaching about the Lord." Do we pray expectantly, in the hope that God will at times validate the truth of the gospel with acts of power or words of knowledge or prophecy?

- Much of the issue of evangelism comes down to believers learning some simple basics. Do we pray for our friends regularly? This is as much for our own hearts as it is to see God move them to openness. Do we prioritize relational time with people who don't know Jesus? Time spent with non-Christians communicates that we value them, and this often leads them to feel safe enough to ask questions and be vulnerable. Do we strategically position our Christian friends within our networks? The gospel is then seen and heard through the lives of a group and not only through us as individuals. Do we ask each other questions about faith? This provides us the opportunity to know what our authentic and personal response could be if/when our non-Christian friends ask. Finally, have we identified one or two gifted evangelists on our team? We need to pray for their ministries and integrate them into the opportunities God is providing the body.

Debrief: *Wow, so* initiating *involves quite a lot of important activities! We discern and decide how we can best sow God's* **shalom** *in ways that are healthy, strategic, and sustainable. We organize ourselves to sensitively demonstrate and proclaim good news in Christ's name, while also beginning to practice communion, community, and mission. As our church planting team practices the* **initiate** *dynamic, we'll find greater freedom as we follow Jesus into mission in our local context. And, there will be the fruit of a growing base of relationships moving in the direction of Jesus, with some - Lord willing - deciding to bow the knee to Christ for the first time.*

 **MAP It!**

Turn to your Missional Action Plan in Appendix A. Go to the *Initiate* section listed under *Strategy*. Review with your team the questions you find there in light of all of your work on the exercises in this chapter. Write down three initiating activities your team will commit to.

My Thoughts on *Initiating*:

What questions do you still have about initiate?

How will you approach culture differently?

What did you learn about evangelism that you did not know before?

If you had to rate your comfort with evangelism on a scale of one to ten, ten being the most comfortable and one being the least, how would you rate yourself?

What worked well for you in this chapter? What are you excited to do?

What needs to be changed? What are you avoiding?

What is your takeaway from this chapter?

PART THREE - GOING DEEP: FORMING WHO WE ARE

*With the **embed** and **initiate** dynamics activated, we're well on our way to becoming a community that is able to intentionally demonstrate and proclaim the gospel. We've created ways for people to belong and to participate alongside us as they explore who Jesus is and the difference He makes in our lives. We're operating as a missional community with enough momentum to challenge each other to grow toward God and one another. At this stage the time is ripe to dig deep and agree on our communal identity and way of life together, so that we can not only form as a sustainable community but also be formed as a people who think, act, and care like Jesus. The perspectives, activities, and structured processes that help us deepen discipleship and begin the long journey of maturing as a healthy church are the dynamics of **practice** and **mature**. These dynamics, which are covered in the next two chapters, enable our spiritual community to grow toward the stature of an accessible, self-governing, and self-supporting church.*

Chapter 5 - Practice: Expressing Our Unique Identity

 As we continue to engage our context through **embedding** *and* **initiating**, *it's very likely that we will find ourselves collecting a small community. As church planters, our natural instinct might be to make our project "official" by starting up a worship service. For now, we urge you to resist that instinct. There's a little more work to be done first. And that work is critical at this stage - understanding who we are, who we want to become, and how we'll get there. We need to establish our communal identity. In this chapter, we'll lead you through numerous exercises to help you sort through all the issues related to identity: your vision, values, beliefs, core metaphor, and perhaps even help you name your community. From there we'll help you do what is often overlooked: we'll guide your team to develop and adopt spiritual practices and rhythms that encourage you to truly be who you say you are. This is exciting and important work, learning to express your unique signature as a distinct local body of believers!*

PRACTICE - *express the identity and Jesus life you're inviting others into*

At this point, you might be thinking: Okay, we spend a good amount of our time and energy living like local missionaries. We're growing in our understanding of our city, and as insiders, we've found ways to keep our fingers on the pulse of local culture. We know our neighbors by name, and we do life together. Occasionally we serve alongside them. We're learning to be better listeners than tellers, while at the same time we don't shy away from appropriately sharing Jesus as God prompts us. And we've organized ourselves enough as a team to make informed decisions about when and how frequently we meet, what we do when we come together, and how to steward this *thing* that we're doing that's become a spiritual community in its own right.

So, what's next? Isn't this the time where we notch it up and focus more effort on developing our gathered life? If *embed* and *initiate* are about activating a gospel-sowing presence *"out there,"* isn't it time to create a compensating anyone-can-come worship gathering that feeds us *"in here"*?

What *Practicing* Means and Why It's So Important

Well, it may be a good time to start gathering more formally and regularly as an accessible community, but that will depend on a host of factors that relate to your team's unique situation. We in Communitas think that at this stage there are more important activities to give our attention to than shifting our focus toward developing a large group worship gathering. There are two reasons for this. For one, it is critical for teams to keep fueling the *embed* and *initiate* dynamics among their wider core group. This takes ongoing time and attention. We can't just *embed* and *initiate* once and think we're done. However, we believe there is even more important work we ought to pour our energies into at this stage. Team leadership must now help the forming spiritual community to agree on and act out who it is, what it stands for, where it's going, and what disciplines or rhythms will shape its life as a people.

Communitas labels these activities with the action word *practice*. We choose this verb because at this stage the community must invest in practicing or living into two signature elements: 1) its unique communal identity - who it wants to be as a distinct local body with Jesus as the Head; and 2) its pattern of discipleship - what it wants its members to do together to help them think, act, and care like Jesus. These two key elements act like glue to help the community hold together as it navigates change, conflict, and the influx of new people with their own ideas on who a group should be and what they should do.

Communal identity includes the *being* aspects of our team's vision, values, name, theological stance, etc. It is different from those general aspects of identity we talked about in chapter one that apply to all Christians - our personal identity as beloved children of God, and our general identity or calling in the world to be creators and cultivators of God's *shalom*. Again, communal identity relates to *our unique signature as a distinct local body of believers.*

Our pattern of discipleship, on the other hand, includes that defined set of practices or rhythms we choose to positively shape or form us as we practice them over time.

Now, you may be saying to yourself, "Yes, of course, practicing is important. But it's not really that difficult to come up with some nicely worded documents that capture the elements of our identity and our spiritual disciplines." This is very true! It is easy to browse the websites of successful churches or cutting edge church plants, and cut and paste our way to the perfect description of who we want to be and how we will disciple people. What's not so easy is actually living into or experimenting with that identity and way of life. This is precisely why so many leadership teams do the defining part well while choosing to skip the actual *practicing* of what they've defined.

This is why Communitas emphasizes *practice* as a key dynamic in missional church planting. Teams need to "walk the walk," to experience what it means to *practice* an identity and way of life before they can credibly ask others to step into that communal journey of being and doing. Otherwise, they become salespersons for an identity and way of life that they are not yet living. Values, vision, name, theology, spiritual disciplines, etc. - these are all elements that mean something because they've been contoured by actually living into them as a group. How can we claim these have meaning for us and transform us if we ourselves have not road-tested them?

In the early stages of a community's formation, the core team will need only to cast a basic set of identity statements and frame only a simple pattern of discipleship practices. However, the elements and practices that make up our communal identity and discipleship pattern will need to be monitored and amended over time, since the church is a living organism that needs to adapt to keep its direction, values, beliefs, and practices consistent with the goal of making more and better disciples.

The Quest to Describe Who We Are (Our Communal Identity)

Practicing our unique group identity may not sound that important to you right now. But whatever clarity and unity we can come to over vision, values, core beliefs, and even the name we choose to call ourselves will serve us greatly as we move into the future. For one thing, people will have the information they need to decide whether or not they fit our community (and vice versa). That clarity and unity will also provide us with a way to evaluate which ministry opportunities and partnerships our team ought to pursue amid a host of possibilities.

Another great advantage of clearly defining our group's identity relates to leadership. With a clear view (in writing) of who the community intends to be, leaders are able to serve the group by keeping the ministry, activities, and way of operating within the sphere of that agreed-upon identity. These agreements bond the community together so that leaders don't have to spend all their time trying to hold people together. As spiritual writer and business guru Margaret Wheatley puts it:

"[It has been said] that the primary task of being a leader is to make sure that the organization knows itself. That is, we must realize that our task is to call people together often, so that everyone gains clarity about who we are, who we've just become, who we still want to be. This includes the

interpretations available from our customers, our markets, our history, our mistakes. If the organization can stay in a continuous conversation about who it is and who it is becoming, then leaders don't have to undertake the impossible task of trying to hold it all together."[35]

Although Wheatley is addressing business organizations, her advice is just as relevant to communities desiring to form sustainable churches. In its own journey of church planting, Eucharist San Francisco, a Communitas partner church, discovered how important it is to give attention to its identity formation. Ryan Jones, founding pastor of Eucharist, shares a bit of their community's process of coming to grips with who they want to be:

When we got started in the Bay area, we expected our greatest challenges to be financial in nature, given the cost of living in San Francisco. Limited finances to meet personal and ministry needs have been cause for moments of anxiety, but I can safely say that finances haven't been our biggest challenge. To our surprise, virtually all of our challenges have been related to gathering a strong core group with an aligned sense of mission, culture, and vision, including some mature leaders who share this alignment.

We found this challenge surprising because we initially put so much thought into mission, vision, and our intended church culture even before we touched down in San Francisco. We had spent months processing our theological and missional foundations and thought we had a strong sense of identity. We also had pretty thoroughly thought through our sense of vision for the church before we ever hit the ground. We did our best not to be grandiose. We kept ourselves firmly focused on what "kind" of church we would be rather than specifics about what our

35 Margaret Wheatley, "Goodbye, Command and Control," http://margaretwheatley.com/wp-content/uploads/2014/12/Goodbye-Command-and-Control.pdf (accessed 15 September 2016).

church would look like (size, buildings, specialized ministries, type of person we would reach, etc.). All this legwork, however, did not prepare us adequately for the challenge of road-testing that identity and sense of calling in real life.

Our journey so far has led me to believe that many of the most important identity questions cannot be adequately understood apart from the various crises or conflicts a congregation faces. These crises help a church define itself more clearly and deeply. And, in order to prevent such crises from becoming destructive, every church needs to wrestle with them against the backdrop of an intentionally defined sense of direction and theological framework.

As I look back over the past few years, the major challenges and defining seasons we as a community have worked through were all about identity in some way or another. Here are some questions we have wrestled with or currently are wrestling with at Eucharist that are proving relevant to our quest to understand our identity more clearly:

- *How do we relate to and define for ourselves the authority of the scriptures?*
- *How do we relate to tradition and the historic teaching of the Church?*
- *How do we relate to emotion in our church life and in spiritual formation?*
- *How do we relate to other churches and Christians? (Fundamentalists, Evangelicals, Mainline Protestants, Catholics, and Orthodox)*
- *How do we relate to non-Christians who interact with our community? (Seekers, skeptics, the hostile, the apathetic, etc.)*
- *How do we, as members of a local community, relate to one another? (Conflict, emotional transparency, expectations, accountability, structure vs. spontaneity, etc.)*
- *How do we relate to questions about personal autonomy vs. group identity? (Individualism vs. collectivism)*
- *How do we relate to controversial social issues?*

(Sexuality, politics, finances, etc.)

Our mission statement has also been a rallying point for us: "to make apprentices of Jesus who become full accomplices in the Story of God." Similarly, our name, Eucharist, has been a wonderful symbolic image holding us to our sense of calling and summarized in our motto: "learning to embody the hospitality of God." And, in like manner, we have found our "culture document" very grounding for us as a community.

Our identity has been strengthened by our choice to root ourselves in the Christian calendar and its seasons (which flowed out of our uneasiness about not being in communion with the wider Church around the world and in history). Our choice to root ourselves in a particular geographical part of San Francisco has also been additive for our identity. We recently clarified for ourselves that our primary missional focus is to be a church for the people within an approximately one-mile radius of our building in downtown San Francisco. This radius heightens and focuses our sense of calling.

As part of their development, the Eucharist community needed to wrestle with who they want to be as a people. The church community recently decided to root themselves in the Anglican tradition, so the way they practice continues to be refined. Their entire quest of self-discovery has been a long process, and not without pain. But now the church has tightened and freshened those elements around which they center themselves. This will help the young, maturing church walk in unity through the season of development ahead.

So what are some processes we can use to help define some of the more important elements of community identity? Below you will find a series of exercises to help you define your group's values, vision, metaphor or name, and core beliefs. Your team might find it helpful to take time away in a retreat setting to work through this series of exercises in sequence.

Defining Church Values

Time: 2 to 4 hours depending on method and team size
Supplies: Whiteboard and markers, sticky-notes, pens or pencils

What are values? Values are enduring ideals shared by the members of a faith community, those deeply held convictions about what matters most to the group - what they will fight for, what they will lose sleep over in order to protect or achieve. In Appendix I you'll find a team process for drafting your initial set of community values. The value statements you draft as a team should be used for this exercise.

Because shared values are essential to the health of a faith community, we recommend that you work through this exercise twice; first with your core leadership team, and then with your leadership team joined by others from the wider faith community. The gathered group will come to understand that they are helping to more clearly describe the shared values of the church, which will be finalized by the leadership team and representatives from the faith community at large.

1. The facilitator describes to the group what values are, why shared church values are important, and why this exercise is important. She gives some examples of church values and explains that the leadership team has already done a draft run on describing potential values that today's work will be integrated into.

2. In small groups, discuss what your faith community values. Come up with a list of at least six values. Then write each of the values on a sticky-note, ranking each one according to importance, with #1 being the most important, #6 being the least.

3. Back as a large group, each small group presents their values and posts them on the whiteboard. Arrange the values together on the whiteboard according to their number rating. All the #1's will be together, then the #2's, and so on.

4. Once everyone has posted their values, regroup the values according to theme within the numbered categories. For example, "honesty" and "integrity" might be similar enough to be grouped together. Feel free to move the values from one number category to another if it seems appropriate.

5. The larger group decides on four to eight values to be taken into consideration as guiding values for your church. The larger group can flesh them out with explanations, Bible verses, images, stories, etc. as much as they consider necessary.

6. The leadership team and several members of the faith community agree to take this conversation further and compare and contrast the leadership team's values draft with that of the combined large group. The two drafts are synthesized into a church values final draft.

NOTE: Make sure you capture what you intend to help your faith community actually live out. Too many values statements end up with one or more values that remain latent or inactive. As a team, you're after *actual values* not *aspirational values*. This is why a faith community must road-test or practice whatever they define as values to verify them as *actual* values.

Defining Church Vision

Time: 4 hours
Supplies: Blank paper, pens or pencils, sticky-notes, whiteboard and markers, list of values from **Defining Church Values** *exercise*

What is vision? A vision is a picture that one has in their mind that demonstrates where a community or individual wants to be in the future. By this stage of your community's development, the core team already has some sense of that preferred future the group is heading toward - and this needs to be described in writing by the team.

As with the previous exercise **Defining Church Values** a church's vision is so important that we recommend you work through this exercise twice; first with your core leadership team, and then with your leadership team joined by others from the wider faith community. The gathered group will come to understand that they are helping to more clearly describe the vision of the church, which will be finalized by the leadership team and representatives from the faith community at large.

Create an environment with no distractions. Provide each person with a piece of notebook paper and pen. Post or hand out the list of the values determined in the previous exercise **Defining Church Values**.

1. In small groups, each small group claims a community value from the list. Individuals write the value on the top of their papers and then add the vision he or she has for living out that value in community. What are the outcomes you would hope to accomplish? What would it look like? You may do this in narrative, paragraph form, or in bullet points. Take ten minutes for this process.

    When time is up everyone passes their paper to the person on their left. That person gets five minutes to read, comment on, or add to it. After five minutes again pass the papers to the left. Repeat the process until the papers return to their original owners.

2. Within your small group, develop a short paragraph that describes how that value could be lived out in community as part of your vision. This will come from the creative writing in step one. Write the vision on a sticky-note.

3. The facilitator convenes the large group. When prompted, each small group tells their value, then posts their vision on the whiteboard and reads it aloud to the group. After each presentation the large group is encouraged to ask clarifying questions. Repeat this process until all values/visions are presented.

4. The facilitator groups the notes by value. Then the group collaboratively creates vision statements for each value represented.

5. A volunteer compiles all of the value/vision statements on the whiteboard. These represent your unique version of the values that will shape the vision for your church.

6. The leadership team and several members of the faith community agree to take this conversation further and compare and contrast the leadership team's draft vision statement with that of the combined large group. The two drafts are synthesized into a final draft of the church vision statement.

Choosing a Name or Core Metaphor

Time: 3 hours
Supplies: Whiteboard and markers

What is a metaphor? A metaphor is one thing conceived as representing another; it is a symbol. For example when Jesus said, "I am the bread of life" he wasn't claiming to be a loaf of bread. He intended us to realize that He is our sustenance. Metaphors can be full of deep and powerful meaning; the metaphors we use to describe ourselves often shape the way we see ourselves, and the way others see us too. Church names such as The Well, Oasis, and Decoupage are interesting examples of well-chosen, contextually meaningful metaphors.

1. Think of all the metaphors that you have used for your team or church. The facilitator writes them on the whiteboard. What names have people from outside of your community given you? List any Biblical imagery or stories that have been significant for your team. If you have no names, brainstorm for five minutes and come up with a list. What do you like or dislike about each of them?

2. With your team, respond to these questions:
    *   *How do you want your church to be known in the wider community?*
    *   *What image do you want your members to hold in their minds for a church identity?*
    *   *What image do you want outsiders to associate with your church? What kind of metaphor supports your team values (see previous exercise)?*
    *   *Is it more important to you to name your church for those who are Christians and in the church already, or for those still outside of it?*

Examples of church named to please those already within the church (shop-talk): Theophilus, Imago Dei, Eucharist, Agape Church, Mars Hill, The King's Temple, Bread and Wine, Parish Collective, Shabbat, Solomon's Porch, etc.

Examples of churches named to draw in those from outside (beacon): The Porch Light, The Front Porch, The Bridge, The Refuge, Food Church, Underground, Home, The Jesus Church, The Anchor, etc.

What do you notice about the shop-talk names as opposed to beacon names?

3. Decide which kind of metaphor you prefer for your church. Try to come up with one that is meaningful for those already part of the church and also acts as a beacon of hope for those outside who will come.

4. Develop a short list of metaphors for your faith community. The facilitator writes them on the whiteboard. Take a few minutes to say each metaphor aloud. Talk about your faith community using the metaphor. For each specific metaphor respond to these questions:
    - *What are the implications of the metaphor?*
    - *Does it connect with your values?*
    - *How does it apply uniquely to you?*
    - *How is it semantically? Does it sound too much like something else?*
    - *Does it have a usable image?*
    - *Does it feel like you?*
    Eliminate any metaphor that doesn't make the grade.

5. Erase the comprehensive list and write the new short list on the whiteboard. From those that remain use your team discernment process to select a guiding metaphor and/or name.

As we conclude this series of learning exercises, we want to focus your attention on the critical subject of core beliefs. A core belief is a belief that is so integral to the system that without it the system will crumble. While the preceding exercises in this series have touched on core beliefs at some level, none rise to the magnitude of core theological beliefs. Personal theological beliefs are often deeply held and above compromise. Yet our teams are comprised of individuals who rarely find themselves in perfect theological alignment. The following exercises are intended to help your team define a basic set of core beliefs, but note that the first in the series is an exercise to discern and process conflict. We believe this is the proper place to start such an important task. We encourage you to engage these exercises prayerfully, humbly, and patiently. Be ready to spend all the time you need for these two exercises.

Discerning Conflicts Over Core Beliefs

Time: 2 hours
Supplies: Copies of Appendix J, pens or pencils

1. Individuals read Appendix J and underline those items on the list they deem absolutely necessary for Christian practice. Write in additional statements if necessary.

2. With a partner compare your results and discuss those areas in which you disagree. Use the following prompts:
   - *Where are your tension points?*
   - *How will you navigate them?*
   - *How will failing to deal with these tensions threaten the viability of a mission or church plant?*

3. Gather as a team. Take turns sharing your experiences with the team. Share your tension points and how you navigated them.

4. After everyone has shared, discuss the following:
   - *What did you learn about yourself?*
   - *How will failing to deal with tensions threaten the viability of the mission?*
   - *How will you handle theological conflict?*

Defining Core Beliefs

Time needed: 90 minutes
Supplies: Sticky-notes, whiteboard and markers, pens or pencils

1. Individuals turn back a few pages in this chapter and review Eucharist's questions concerning understanding its identity. Which questions seem most compelling to you for development of your church? Why?

2. List your personal top five defining core beliefs for Christian practice on sticky-notes, one belief per note. Refer to Appendix J if necessary.

3. Gathered as a team, take turns sharing your core beliefs with the team and post them on the whiteboard.

4. After everyone has shared, the facilitator leads the team in a discussion to arrange the core beliefs in order of importance. Take your time and be sure that everyone is heard.

5. After agreement is reached on the order of importance, the team selects a set of defining core beliefs that work towards theological unity. Record them in your journal for future reference.

Discovering Our Way of Life (Our Group's Pattern of Discipleship)

In September, 1999, Christian leaders from over 54 countries, representing nearly 90 organizations, denominations, and churches, convened in Eastbourne, England, to address the increasing absence of transformative discipleship praxis rampant among churches today. In light of this crisis, their goal was to draft a statement of common commitment—call it a manifesto of sorts. Over the course of four days, the statement was revised six times to reflect more than one hundred comments and recommendations from the diverse group. The result was compelling. They stated:

"As we face the new millennium, we acknowledge that the state of the Church is marked by a paradox of growth without depth. Our zeal to go wider has not been matched by a commitment to go deeper. Researchers and pollsters have documented the fact that many times:

1. *Christians are not that different from the culture around them. When the desert wind blows, it shapes the sand, and the Church has become more like the sand than the wind.*
2. *We grieve that many within the Church are not living lives of biblical purity, integrity, and holiness. The need is in the pulpit and pew alike.*
3. *The lack of true discipleship has resulted in a lack of power in the Church to impact our culture."[36]*

Communitas believes that the way we practice our faith ought to change us for the good. As missional initiatives and churches are multiplied across many continents, we desire to see growth *with* depth. We realize that this will not happen without teams having a firm and enduring commitment to the *practice* dynamic.

"Throughout the history of the church," author and historian Alan Roxburgh notes, "we discover local communities shaped by practices of life or disciplines that cause them to stand out and cause others to take heed. [These communities] learned to live as a contrast society shaped by [such practices as] hospitality, radical forgiveness, the breaking down of social and racial barriers, and self-sacrificial love."[37] As we live inside God's story, these habits of life empower us to give the world a taste of this Kingdom of God that is coming.

Community identity is one critical aspect of the *practice* dynamic. But the other side of the same coin has to do with the pattern of discipleship a group decides to live under. Teams need to experiment with their chosen rhythms and disciplines and amend or change aspects of them along the way so that they're achieving their goal of shaping you as a people. Here's a story of how Decoupage in Madrid, Spain, has fleshed out the *practice* dynamic. As you read, note the elements of identity formation and those activities that became spiritual rhythms for the group.

---

36 Troy Cady and Amy Swacina (drawing from *Ancient Future Evangelism*, by Robert Webber), "Discipleship as Sacramental Living," in *Grow Where You're Planted: Collected Stories on the Hallmarks of Maturing Church* (Portland: Christian Associates Press, 2013), 84.

37 Alan J. Roxburgh and M. Scott Boren, *Introducing the Missional Church: What It Is, Why It Matters, How to Become One* (Grand Rapids: Baker, 2009), 105.

April Te Grootenhuis Crull offers us the account:

In 2007, Kelly and I expressed where we felt God was leading us to start a missional initiative into a very specific neighborhood, Malasaña, to do a type of ministry that was focused on radical commitment to each other and to daily living among our neighbors. As we shared this vision with others, three people decided to join our missional initiative team.

In the first year of our team, as we committed to embedding, we also wrestled with each other to understand our practice of following Jesus. We came from a diversity of settings and shared the common goal for our community to reflect the culture in which we found ourselves. First we analyzed the values and mission statement that Kelly and I had initially written, revising and rewriting as we attempted to agree on the concepts. Next, we asked ourselves, what does it truly mean to be a church together? We settled on the ideas of Formation, Worship, Community, and Mission centered around Jesus Christ. In a picture we overlaid these concepts on our neighborhood map and we began to develop rhythms that fulfilled these different areas, with lots of experimentation. For example, initially we had a daily prayer time at the central plaza in Malasaña, reflecting a neighborhood rhythm of gathering over drinks there at the end of the day.

As we realized this commitment level was not sustainable for bi-vocational team members, it eventually became three times a week, then once a week, until we realized it really did not serve our community or our intentions. We also developed a weekly spiritual discussion group that included a meal together, which was modeled on a neighborhood habit of discussion groups. This format, and even the time we hold meeting, has continued since we started. Even though we have tried various iterations, we have returned time and again to this rhythm. The participative nature of this group has been consistently challenged by newcomers and consistently chosen by the community. In the first year, we also had a weekly leadership development meeting that eventually decreased in frequency, as our shared vision grew deeper.

Our church was founded on a strong prioritization of members living in or spending significant amounts of time in Malasaña. Connected to this identity arose the question of what made our developing church unique from other churches and also how Christians from other churches would relate to us. We chose to encourage Christians already involved in a church to find inspiration from us, but to stay committed to their current church.

We also wrestled with theology. In the first few months of our project our first son was born and our community had to wrestle with our views and practice of baptism, and as a result our process of engaging core theological concepts, conflicts, and each other was developed. Following this process, we soon examined our beliefs about tithing and the need (or not) of holding money in common, which prompted our process of deciding how to use this money as a community on mission. Our artist in residence program was birthed from this question of tithing, based on our experiences of embedding and initiating. Reflecting on these conversations and times of wrestling reveals that not only was the result concepts and words that we chose to commit to as a community, but truly creating the culture and practice of the process we use to make decisions and live them out together.

A few years into our project, as the community continued to grow little by little, we met with a missional community in another part of Spain. They shared about one of their practices called grupos de crecimiento, in which two or three people would meet weekly to ask each other a list of accountability questions. We recognized the relevance of this practice for our culture and decided to give it a try. Within weeks, the men's group was finding great growth and joy in this discipleship practice. The women's group took various restarts over a few years before it was able to find a way that worked for them.

The following exercise will help you examine the real-world journey of Decoupage (above) as they developed a communal way of life.

Understanding Practice *in Action*

Time: 45 minutes - Supplies: Journal, whiteboard and markers, pens or pencils

1. Individually: In Decoupage's story above, underline patterns of discipleship that were developed.

2. Gathered as the team, discuss Decoupage's core practices. Note key insights on the whiteboard. Use the following prompts:
   - *What did they "do?"*
   - *How does this story resonate with your own group practices?*
   - *How does it challenge you?*
   - *What do they inspire you to "do?"*

3. Record your thoughts in your journal. Underline potential action items for you and your team.

Different churches in different cultures have identified core patterns of discipleship. As we might expect, their patterns of discipleship differ, too. Although there is universality to the patterns, each individual church expresses them in unique ways. Some churches call them spiritual formation, while others call them discipleship, teaching, spiritual disciplines, rhythms, or rules of life. Whatever the name, what we are referring to here are behaviors that mold our spirit and actions to look more like Jesus.

Inagrace Dietterich identifies five general categories of practices the church, historically, has commonly engaged in:

1. Baptism – joining and sharing
2. Breaking bread – eating and drinking
3. Reconciliation – listening and caring
4. Discernment – testing and deciding, and,
5. Hospitality – welcoming and befriending.[38]

Dorothy Bass and Craig Dykstra argue for another specific set of practices:

"Honoring the body, hospitality, household economics, saying yes and saying no, keeping sabbath, testimony, discernment, shaping communities, forgiveness, healing, dying well, singing our lives – woven together, these constitute a way of life. Each of these practices could be found somewhere in the life of every Christian congregation."[39]

Elements of discipleship will naturally grow in complexity as a church matures and has greater resources to invest into the spiritual formation of its members. However, maintaining the simplicity of discipleship practice is wise. There are two important reasons to maintain simplicity. For one, simplicity allows as many members as possible to meaningfully engage in a common life. At the same time, outsiders

---

38 Darrell L. Guder, ed., "Missional Community: Cultivating Communities of the Holy Spirit," in *Missional Church: A Vision for the Sending of the Church in North America* (Grand Rapids: Wm. B. Eerdmans, 1998), 153-182.

39 Dorothy C. Bass and Craig Dykstra, "Christian Practices and Congregational Education in Faith," www.practicingourfaith.org/pdf/Christian%20Practices%20&%20Congregational%20Education.pdf (accessed 10 November 2016).

have an easy inroad into the life of a faith community. Both Christian and non-Christian newcomers can begin to participate in the rhythms of the church before they become stakeholders. As mentioned earlier, they are able to not only *belong* before they believe, but they can also *behave* before they believe.

Smallboatbigsea, a missional church in Sydney, Australia, captures its core practices in a simple pattern it calls BELLS, which is an acronym for five key habits that make up the community's rhythm of life in Christ. A number of church plants around the world have adopted this pattern as an initial way to get the ball rolling on rehearsing a discipleship rhythm. The pattern is defined as follows:

BELLS means that on a weekly basis, smallboatbigsea members covenant to:

B = Bless (practicing generosity & grace) – *I will bless three people this week, at least one of whom is not a member of our church.* The word 'blessing' in ancient Hebrew can simply mean: 'to affect, for good.' We regularly acknowledge the beauty and generosity of God, allowing that grace to overflow to others. We look for ways to 'affect people for good;' from being generous, adding value to our neighborhood, to recognizing and affirming the Imago Dei in someone. All of these are gifts given without expectation.

E = Eat & Drink (practicing fellowship & hospitality) – *I will eat with three people this week, at least one of whom is not a member of our church.* Just as Jesus built community around table fellowship, we regularly eat & drink with both friends and 'strangers' – whether it's a cup of coffee, a glass of wine, or a meal- noticing God's presence in that moment. We have regular community dinners, as well as practice The Lord's Table together weekly.

L = Listen (practicing silence & attentiveness) – *I will spend at least one period of the week listening to the Spirit's voice.* We strive to be a listening community: listening to God, the voices of others, and the longings of our neighborhood. This happens in our gatherings though hearing Scripture, liturgical prayers, hearing someone's story, in silence, listening walks around our neighborhood, personal prayer practices, and several other ways.

L = Learn (practicing discovery & growth) – *I will spend at least one period of the week learning Christ.* We regularly engage in learning that encourages and stretches our faith... seeing the spiritual life as a continuing journey of transformation. This happens in our gatherings through reading Scripture, and interactive discussion, teaching, and experiences.

S = Sent (practicing being rooted & releasing) – *I will journal throughout the week all the ways I alerted others to the universal reign of God through Christ.* From using our passions and gifts for the good of others, simple do-able acts of compassion, to partnering with others in our city towards the common good; we see SBBS as a sent community. And whether empowering leaders for ministry, seeding new projects & faith communities, or using our resources for the good of others (rather than big programs and big productions); we want to be regularly sending.[40]

Some churches tie their spiritual practices into the basic church commitments of Communion, Community, and Mission. These UP, IN and OUT commitments are a natural framework on which to hang a community's core practices.

---

40 Michael Frost, *Surprise the World: The Five Habits of Highly Missional People* (Colorado Springs: Navpress, 2016), 22.

Churches also develop different forms of account- ability. One movement has followed monastic groups of old in developing a "Rule of Life." Trevor Miller of the Northumbria Community expands on this concept, noting what his semi-monastic community means when they use the word "rule":

A Rule is a means whereby, under God, we take responsibility for the pattern of our spiritual lives. It is a 'measure' rather than a 'law'. The word 'rule' has bad connotations for many, implying restrictions, limitations and legalistic attitudes. But a Rule is essentially about freedom. It helps us to stay centered, bringing perspective and clarity to the way of life to which God has called us. The word derives from the Latin regula, which means 'rhythm, regularity of pattern, a recognizable standard' for the conduct of life. Esther De Waal has pointed out that 'regula is a feminine noun which carried gentle connotations' rather than the harsh negatives that we often associate with the phrase 'rules and regulations' today... A Rule is an orderly way of existence but we embrace it as a way of life not as keeping a list of rules. It is a means to an end – and the end is that we might seek God with authenticity and live more effectively for Him.[41]

Other churches find it helpful to tie specific per- sonal questions to each practice. Questions invite participants to wrestle each week with how they're going to apply this practice to their own situation. For example, if we were to define one of our practices as *regularly applying Scripture to our lives*, some questions we might ask ourselves would be: When will I (we) take the time to listen to Scripture together in the week ahead? Who will join us in this reflecting, and how will we ensure that we're actually applying what we're learning? How will we take advantage of the stories of transformation in our midst that encourage us to stay engaged with Scripture?

As aids to applying the practices we're experiment- ing with, many churches, both young and older, find dyads or triads (same gender groups of two or three people) a helpful way to keep people motivated and growing in a common discipleship rhythm. Small groups can be helpful too, but there's often no sub- stitute for the intimacy of groups of two or three to provoke accountability, vulnerability, and progress toward change.

In summary, there are many ways to shape a rule of life for your faith community; the options are nearly endless. The practices you adopt should reflect the uniqueness of your church and its context. The most essential element, however, is that you and your team truly commit to a set of spiritual practices you will exercise together. Your community's rule of life will likely be the foundation of your discipleship, serving to bring the people closer to God, closer to one another, and more invested in their sense of purpose in the world. We suggest a pattern that correlates to the three elemental functions of church - Communion, Community, and Mission (CCM). The next exercise will help your team develop a rule of life around the three elements.

---

41   Trevor Miller, "What is a Rule of Life?" www.northumbri- acommunity.org/who-we-are/our-rule-of-life/what-is-a- rule-of-life/ (accessed 9 December 2007).

Identifying Your Community's Spiritual Practices/Rule of Life

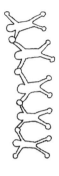

Time: 90 minutes

*Supplies: Six foot long (2 meter) by two to three feet wide (1 meter) piece of paper and markers. The paper can be taped together using newsprint or butcher paper. Copies of Values and Vision documents developed in earlier exercises (see chapter five), practices from the exercise **Addressing Imbalances in Culture** in chapter four, whiteboard and markers, paper, tape, pens or pencils*

1. Individually: Review the general discipleship practices described in the section above (both general historic practices and the BELLS rhythm). On individual sticky-notes, write three to five practices that you think might be appropriate for your team to experiment with in this season ahead. One practice per sticky-note.

2. Each person shares with the team their practices, posting their notes on the whiteboard and explaining what they've written. As the sharing progresses, the facilitator notes where there is overlap with what has already been mentioned.

3. As a team, review the Values and Vision documents you devised earlier. Underline the five or six phrases that seem most critical to you in your discipleship practices. Compare these phrases to the list on the whiteboard. If any practices are missing, write them on sticky-notes and post them on the whiteboard.

4. In small groups of four or less, consider your local culture and context:
    *   Identify a few ways that your local culture is advocating for a lifestyle that promotes community health and godly values. What scriptures support these practices? Write each practice and its scripture reference on a sticky-note.
    *   Review the practices you arrived at in the exercise on **Addressing Imbalances in Culture** in the previous chapter. Write on sticky-notes any practices that might help your community respond where culture is damaging people.

5. Gather as a team. When prompted, each small group posts their sticky-notes on the whiteboard and reads them aloud. Compare each new sticky-note to the current whiteboard list, adding any practice that is missing and important to your team's spiritual practice.

6. A volunteer allows herself to be traced on the large sheet of paper in black marker with arms uplifted. The team evaluates the sticky-notes with practices and categorizes each of them, moving each practice to the image of the body:
    *   On the uplifted hands, place practices that bring you into closer Communion with God.
    *   On the chest, place practices that disciple our hearts and strengthen the bonds of Community between us.
    *   On the legs and feet, place practices that impact lives through Mission.

- If a practice applies to a few areas, indicate this by connecting the practices to the areas that apply with black marker. Overlap is good!

7. Hang your picture on the wall. Step back and review it. Then read over each contribution and decide by consensus those practices you wish to adopt as a rule of life for your church. Prioritize those that align most closely with your vision, those that apply in one or more areas, and those that are invitational to folks who are not a part of your church. Record your practices in your journal for future reference.

As you've no doubt seen by now, developing a core identity and discipleship pattern is difficult and time-consuming work. It is, however, crucial work that pays dividends in the current and future life of your community. Even though you may have worked through the many exercises in this chapter, your team may not be completely satisfied that you've fully captured the language and practices that define your uniqueness. We want to encourage you to keep at it! This is a process involving creativity, experimentation, and patient road-testing of your ideas to arrive at the right identity statements and practices for your community. We also suggest that you review them periodically. They may need to be altered as your community grows and deepens.

Debrief: *Coming into agreement over the two vital issues of 'being' and 'doing' represents some of the most important work a planting team will engage in. Through identity formation and development of a discipleship pattern, the forming community begins to fully inhabit the spiritual house it has built, and it invites others to live there too. The team can boldly invite others to live out this identity and rhythm of life, since they themselves have begun to find it transformative. Some experimenting with identity and way of life has no doubt been occurring before this* **practice** *phase, but here it is intentionally passed on through the core community (i.e. the project's stakeholders). The* **practice** *phase prepares the church to eventually "throw open the doors," project its public face, and invite others into the long journey of maturing as a local church.*

This work will be revisited many times over the life of the project. So, as is the case with **embed** *and* **initiate,** *the* **practice** *dynamic is not only relevant to a project startup but also to* **maturing** *churches all throughout their life*

.

 **MAP It!**

Turn to your Missional Action Plan in Appendix A. Go to the *Practice* section listed under *Strategy*. Review with your team the questions you find there in light of all of your work on the exercises in this chapter. Write down three practices your team will commit to. Then jump up to the *Vision* section. In light of all the work you've done in this chapter, are there additional thoughts you'd like to record there? Do you need to edit something you've previously written? Finally, revisit the *Basics of Church* section. Record any new thoughts you may have or revise what you've previously written.

My Thoughts on *Practicing*:

What are the questions that you still have about practice?

What worked well for you in this chapter?

Which parts were more difficult to grasp and why?

What needs to be addressed that is not here?

What was your takeaway thought from this chapter?

CHAPTER 5

Chapter 6 - Mature: Growing Up as a Sustainable Faith Community

 As we've learned, **practicing** *is about discovering through experimentation how a group chooses to express itself as a body of Christ. If we've* **embedded** *and* **initiated** *well, our context has deeply informed the identity of our project, the "who we choose to be together in light of God's call in the neighborhood." As we live into that identity and also engage communal rhythms and activities that form us spiritually, our* **practicing** *together enables us to increasingly become a unique expression of the body of Christ - a community well on the way to becoming a local church.*

Maturing *is the process of developing over time as a unique, local expression of the body of Christ. While* **maturing** *could be seen as merely an extension of practicing, there is more to it than that.* **Maturing** *requires our team to exercise an intentionality not yet present in* **practicing**. *We must collectively make a deeper commitment to become a fuller expression of that identity and purpose we've discerned. This commitment helps ensure the health and sustainability of our project, while also providing the host context greater avenues of access to it.*

MATURE - *develop as a unique, local expression of the body of Christ*

The essence of the *maturing* dynamic is that the church is now taking on a life of its own. The church is in the process of becoming a sustainable community no longer dependent on the dreams of its founders and the actions of the original team. It is growing as a *body* of Christ, a complex unity of new-comers and old-timers who move together and project a public presence in their local setting. With Jesus as the Head, the community's leaders design healthy rhythms and structures that promote the development of each member while enabling each to play their part in mission and ministry. They also take measures to steward the community's public expression as a distinct, communal entity representing and bearing the *presence* of Christ.

In order to move into this dynamic, the church planting team needs to shift from creating sparks to feeding the fire - empowering more and more people to individually and collectively embody Christ in their calling, character, and giftedness. The team no longer bears the burden alone for leading, nurturing, and equipping the community; rather it develops new leaders and promotes a greater owning and sharing of these responsibilities among the body.

Why *Maturing* is Important and What It Requires

Why *Maturing* is So Critical

Maturing churches, whatever their form, help brighten and sustain the witness of the gospel across every area they inhabit. As each local church "grows up" toward the full stature of Christ, it is able to equip more and more people to think, act, and care like Jesus.[42] And as these members operate in harmony together, the body is able to move constructively as a visible, responsive organism, tending both to its own needs and also those of the host context.

The developmental work involved in *maturing* a church also enables it to be a more vivid *sign* and *foretaste* of the renewal of all things that God is bringing - what the biblical writers call the Kingdom of God or New Creation. Churches pulsate brightly as *signs* of that Kingdom when they express such behaviors as sacrificially loving one another, gathering to pray and remind each other of God's story and each one's part in it, celebrating the Lord's Supper and baptisms, and pursuing compassionate service and justice in Jesus' name. These activities (and many more) act like road signs that point people toward a destination - in our case the destination is that Kingdom realm that history is moving toward, where death will be destroyed along with all powers that resist God's loving reign.[43]

Churches often fail to see the importance of this public ministry of pointing to something beyond themselves. They also often neglect an even more critical aspect of what it means to "go public" - inviting local non-Christian neighbors to *taste* the reality of the Kingdom in the midst of God's people. When churches intentionally make themselves accessible and include non-Christians in prayer, in grace community, and in other practices and events where God's Spirit and the Christ-life can be experienced, this can be a highly persuasive witness to the power of the gospel to transform lives.

In these ways and more, *maturing* churches increasingly grow as both light (sign) and salt (foretaste), and thereby strengthen their prophetic witness in their local settings. This is a great reason to take *maturing* seriously, but there are still other good reasons this dynamic is so important to invest in. *Maturing* churches are also able to grow in their capacity to impact their context as *agents* of the Kingdom. Their commitment to discipleship under Jesus enables the fruits of the Spirit to spill out bountifully in all directions, transforming people and enriching neighborhoods and cities. As they seek their *maturing*, the Spirit is able to use that depth and energy to fuel all kinds of initiatives that bless the Kingdom and display God's compassion and justice. Further,

42 Eph. 4:13.

43 I Cor. 15: 20-28.

a commitment to *maturing* often enables churches to develop the communal strength and resilience to seed new missional churches, both near and far.

What Maturing Requires

In Communitas we don't insist that our missional initiatives and projects grow to look like any particular form of church as they *mature*. We do not have one preferred or ideal model in view. Rather, we entrust each team to discern through its own *embedding*, *initiating*, and *practicing* work, the appropriate expression of church for their context. Whatever form a given church takes, however, its leaders will need to continually take deliberate measures to keep their community growing toward its unique potential.

We've consciously used the word "deliberate" above to describe the effort required to *mature* a local church. To be deliberate means we combine intentionality with follow-through across a host of fronts to foster the progressive development of the faith community. It "grows up" to the next level, much like a person might mature when she/he takes concrete steps to aid their own growth. Pastor and psychologist Dr. Hud McWilliams often reminds us that human beings need more than simply good intentions to grow as people. Their development is a product of deliberate action where intention is put into operation by pursuing steps toward specific growth goals and is surrounded with relationships and resources that ensure good follow-through. *Maturing* on a human level requires stepping into growth goals and challenges, with support and accountability to help one stay the course. Choosing passivity or leaving growth to chance, Hud argues, almost invariably leads to stunted development.

If humans require such deliberate activity to grow as individuals, why should we imagine it would be any different for groups of human beings (communities) who want to grow up into the full stature of Christ? We in Communitas stand convinced that our projects and churches must be deliberate in their quest to *mature*. Such development does not come by accident on a human level, nor will it drop from the sky for churches that neglect to go after it.

In any given season, each project and church - in its own unique way - will need to prayerfully define measures to help further develop their community. This applies both to projects in their earliest stages of development and also to churches well along in their development! Maturing in one setting might mean the community implements a process for selecting elders to broaden and deepen the leadership base of the church. In another instance, it might equate to leaders articulating a clear pathway for people to join the community and become stakeholders committed to its development. In still another setting, it might mean the leadership develops Kingdom-minded partnerships with other local churches and organizations that increase the overall impact for Christ in their city. Whatever a team discerns that it will do in a given period, *maturing* will require intentionality and follow through in order to develop the capacities for endurance and impact in their local setting.

As part of that discernment, all *maturing* churches, whether young or more seasoned, will need to pause periodically and get perspective on where they've come from, how they're operating, and where they want to go next. Once ministry rhythms, systems, and structures are established in a particular season, it's too easy to fall into maintenance mode and operate in ways that no longer position the church for long term ministry impact. Engaging the *maturing* dynamic means leadership teams must carve out times to reflect and cast out afresh, so that their communities stay nimble to meet an ever-changing future.

For the remainder of this chapter we want to explore four areas that are particularly important to *maturing* any new or existing faith community. After years of watching various expressions of church emerge from the soil of many cultures, we recognize that this transitional zone, where a community shifts from a simple to a more complex, *maturing* form, requires intentionality around: 1) keeping the vision updated, clear, and inspiring; 2) enabling every member of the body to play their part; 3) developing the depth and capacity of the church's leadership community; and, 4) discerning appropriate progress targets that help *mature* the community for the season at hand.

Keeping the Vision Updated, Clear, and Inspiring

All churches and planting teams need to periodically revisit their vision. We mention it here because we encounter so many cases where communities allow their vision to either become outdated or drop out of view altogether. Because so much hangs upon clarity of vision in terms of its contribution to morale, planning, and keeping a group on track, faith communities must ensure that vision remains relevant and articulated in ways that are both inspiring and clear.

Vision needs to be kept in view on two levels simultaneously - at the general (macro) level and at the specific (micro) level. Together these two ways of seeing provide "depth perception," much as human vision needs both eyes operating to accomplish a full field of clear vision. For a church or church plant to maintain depth perception, they need to cultivate

both an inspiring big-picture view of God's dream for the body of Christ and also a captivating vision of what they dream their community might become for their specific, local setting. Both aspects of vision, the farsighted and the nearsighted, pull the community forward and allow the double dream to become reality in the here and now. Let's explore how each of these might be cultivated over time, starting with the macro vision and then addressing the micro.

Through the storyline and teachings of Scripture, the Spirit paints a wonderfully compelling vision of how beautiful God's Church is meant to be as the Body of Christ in the world. We find that many who step into church planting are driven forward by the desire to improve upon what already exists, rather than by God's dream for the Bride. They've developed a keen sense of what they don't like about the church at large or about the churches they've experienced. In reaction, they develop a hunger to invent almost any kind of alternative community that doesn't have the faults of those churches. This reactive posture isn't bad in itself, but at a certain point it needs to be turned into a forward-looking, positive stance. In other words, pioneers need to spend less time in reactivity against the negatives, and more time nurturing an appreciation for what God declares the church can be.

In your progress through this guidebook so far, you've deepened your appreciation of what the church can become for your context. We've developed the exercise below to help you keep your eyes fixed on a compelling, big-picture vision of what God has called the church to be.

Capturing a Compelling Vision for "The Church Beautiful"

Time: 2 hours in 2 parts
Supplies: Copies of Appendix K, whiteboard and markers, paper, large sheet of paper, pens or pencils

This exercise consists of two parts: Personal Reflection and Team Discussion. We suggest completing the Personal Reflection section prior to your team meeting.

Personal Reflection:

1. Read Dr. Wesley White's short essay "The Church Beautiful" in Appendix K underlining the words, phrases, or concepts that really excite your heart. Note three specific points where Wesley has captured your imagination and circle them.

2. Identify the circled words, phrases, or concepts you have experienced. Note these in your journal along with any other experiences you have had with the church that were encouraging and uplifting.

3. In your journal draw or indicate a visual representation of your positive experiences with the "The Church Beautiful." Add an action word or two for each experience that you have illustrated.

4. Bring your illustration and notes to the team discussion below.

Team Discussion:

1. With your team, take turns sharing your highlights and the three points you most liked in the essay. Explain how "The Church Beautiful" meets your hopes and expectations or surprises you in some way. Share your illustrations of the church beautiful and the action words you used to describe them. Facilitator writes these words on the whiteboard.

2. Categorize the action words on the whiteboard using as many categories as needed. Then choose three action words that will move your group towards practicing "The Church Beautiful." On a sheet of paper that is large enough for all to gather around, create a group sketch or collection of sketches illustrating what these three actions look like in your context, how they will reflect "The Church Beautiful."

In Communitas, we love the church! It is Christ's Bride, and we count it a privilege to be involved in starting communities with such potential for beauty and impact in our world. The exercise above gives you a taste of why we believe it is so enormously important for each expression of the body of Christ to grow up into all that God intends for it. Leadership teams must revisit this general vision periodically and creatively hold it in view before their communities. But teams must also deliberately revisit and creatively recast that other aspect of vision we mentioned earlier, the specific vision they've discerned for their local church in its unique setting. In the busyness of building its internal ministries and responding to the many needs of context, many churches commonly experience "vision drift," meaning they slowly lose sight of their original dream and stray off course. This can result in not only poor stewardship of the church's limited resources and energy, but it also leads to low morale within the church as people forget why they're doing what they're doing. Teams must periodically realign the community with the "original dream," and creatively reframe, and even redirect, that dream as the Spirit leads.

The following story from Remko Dekker, of Crossroads Leiden in the Netherlands, illustrates the importance of revisiting the church's unique vision to aid the further *maturing* of the faith community:

One maturing *challenge we face at this moment relates to a loss of vision in the church. Over the years as the community* has developed, certain areas seem to have taken on a life of their own. They are no longer (consciously) linked to "the community we once dreamed we'd be." A business-as-usual feeling has crept in, leading to people/ministries adopting too much of a maintenance-mode way of operating. Vision leak or drift is common to organizations and churches, but it's always experienced more profoundly when you're in the middle of it. You see how slowly but surely over the years it has crept in.

So, now we feel it's time to revisit that part of our identity and to reconnect with the dream of who we want to be. Early on in our development as a community, we asked every ministry team to translate the overall mission/vision document into a mission/vision for their specific ministry. As we recast that vision of who we want to be, we again want to ask all our teams to revisit that mission/vision and to reconnect with it, rewrite it, and re-dream it for their given ministry.

As you can see from Remko's account above, vision drift "crept in" unnoticed and began to affect all the ministry areas of his church. The leadership team has wisely diagnosed that as a problem, and now it's up to them to help the community take deliberate measures to dream afresh and re-align the church's ministries with that freshly recast vision. We have provided the following exercise for your team or leadership community to review and freshly recast its local vision, as well as to re-align ministries to that updated version.

Re-evaluating and Re-casting Communal Vision and Values

Time: Half or full day retreat
Supplies: Large sheets of paper, markers, copies of the vision and values statements developed in the
Defining Church Values *and* **Defining Church Vision** *learning exercises in chapter five.*

1. Assemble your leadership team and key members of your wider leadership community. Write the name or core metaphor you have adopted for your church or project (as developed in the **Choosing a Name or Core Metaphor** learning exercise in chapter five) on a large sheet of paper and post it on the wall. As a team, reflect on how your community's name speaks to the dream that you have for your church in its local setting. Capture these thoughts on the paper.

2. Distribute the vision and values statements developed in the learning exercises **Defining Church Values** and **Defining Church Vision** from chapter five. Volunteers read the statements to the group.

3. Discuss the following questions among the team, a volunteer records your responses on two large sheets of paper, one paper for vision and another for values:
    *   *Where do you feel the community is living well into its vision and values?*
    *   *Where do you feel the community is falling short of the values and vision you described?*
    *   *If you find that you are falling short in an area, how would you change your vision or values or practices to accommodate this shortfall?*
    *   *What opportunities and needs do you see with greater clarity now?*
    *   *Which ones do you sense the Spirit is drawing you to respond to?*
    *   *What practices do you need to develop to accomplish your hoped-for future?*

4. Post the values sheet on the wall to the left of your name or core metaphor, and the vision sheet to the right. This is your team's "Dream Mosaic." Compare your Dream Mosaic with your original vision and values statements.
    *   *What has changed?*
    *   *What is still true?*
    *   *What if anything shall we do about the differences?*
    Decide what next steps are necessary.

OPTIONAL Next Steps:

1. Elect a working group that will develop and propose amended vision and values statements from the Dream Mosaic material. Set a date for the working group to present the amended vision and values statement to the larger group for revision.

2. Group meets to approve final version.

Enabling Every Member of Our Community to Play Their Part

Through the discerned sharing and demonstrating of Good News (*initiating*), and by living into our unique God-given identity and way of life (*practicing*), we have likely begun to operate as a more cohesive local body of Christ. More people are finding their way into our community and are curious to discover how they might participate. Rather than allowing such folks to float on the fringes and occasionally fill a gap here and there, our team needs to take specific measures to help these interested people play a more enduring part in the whole.

In the *embedding* chapter we walked through an exercise designed to match our team's unique passions and giftings to the needs of context (see the exercise **Matching Our Collective Passions with Culture's Needs**). As part of *maturing* from a simple to a more complex form, we need to expand this kind of process so that every interested person might express his or her unique calling and "giftedness."[44] This must become not only a priority at this transitional stage, but an enduring value for the long haul. Otherwise the local body of Christ will be stunted in its development, unable to grow and function the way God intends.

Leaders will wisely want to cultivate this "every member a minister" value at the earliest stages of their project. Miriam Phillips, executive pastor at Crossroads International Church, shares about how this priority became an enduring value in her community:

When Crossroads International Church of Amsterdam was founded in 1987, Christian Associates [now Communitas] strongly emphasized reproducing church planters and sending out evangelists. The initial team intentionally created a culture of informal leadership mentoring, and later, formal leadership development training. These measures, along with making it a norm to invest in every member's God-given potential, established a dynamic and purposeful context for the development of gifts. This culture has persisted even as its form has changed [over the years] as the church has grown from a single small group meeting in a living room to a community averaging 1,300 people in attendance at its three Sunday services.[45]

Crossroads established a developmental culture across their community, investing first in leaders who in turn invested in the development of all members of the body. Staying true to that value has required their core leadership team to invite more voices to the table as well as empower others to take responsibility for cultivating the various ministries of the church. This stance does not come naturally to those at the helm of a growing community. On the contrary, primary leaders tend to keep their hands in too many ministries for too long, fearing that things will come undone if they let go. This stifles the growth of the church and its ability to make disciples. (A passive human body will not stay healthy very long, nor will a church body!). As Miriam puts it: "The traditional method of recruiting volunteers is often too dependent on church leaders alone. What's more, this method is only marginally effective with people leery of centralized top-down leadership, and tends to be limited by the leadership's vision and management expertise. The notion that the connection between

---

44 We define "giftedness" the way J. Robert Clinton defines it: the summation of one's natural abilities, spiritual gifts and skills.

45 Miriam Phillips, "Releasing People into Their Divine Design," *Grow Where You're Planted,* Eds. Daniel Steigerwald and Kelly Crull (Portland: Christian Associates Press, 2013), 173-4.

volunteers and tasks has to be brokered by the leadership [alone] limits the scope of what is possible."[46]

As churches mature, leaders need to allow space for other leaders and volunteers to responsibly develop the ministries of the church. This of course will require the church to deliberately enable people to both identify and express their God-given design. The learning exercise **Matching Our Collective Passions with Culture's Needs** in chapter three is one way a church might do this. Miriam shares another way to help this happen:

Listening to a person's life story has become a major part of the way we do coaching and mentoring. In a sense, we "exegete" (literally "read out") a person's life to hear what God is saying related to gifting and calling. This task is similar to the way we might exegete Scripture or exegete the surrounding culture.

I've seen many people experience aha-moments as they shared their stories in a small group, especially when themes appeared in a person's own story that they had not noticed before. A leader who championed the start of our deacon ministry shared how in elementary school she was in a girls' club that helped elderly people with errands and chores. A man who told the story of his love for adventure and fixing things at a young age realized that this had prepared him to assist missionaries on the field with basic repairs on a short-term missions trip. People make these realizations when they share their life stories.

When a group of people share their stories, and we notice a unique combination of gifts, talents, and skills lining up to create a new opportunity, we do what we can to connect the relational and organizational dots and start conversations about next steps. It's worth listening to people share their life stories.[47]

Carlton Deal, founding pastor of The Well in Brussels, Belgium, encourages leaders to develop people to minister both within their church community but also in the midst of their everyday worlds:

Normal people have jobs or go to school and are gifted to serve, and perhaps even to lead. This has been a core concept for us in our leadership development: how can we develop the systems and structures of church so that the most amount of ministry can take place through the fewest number of full-time staff? And it was also about mission—the ethos of our community was to be about sending [people].

Two verses from Ephesians repeatedly stirred our hearts. First, verse 2:10, which says, "For we are God's workmanship, created in Christ Jesus for good works which he has prepared in advance for us to do." What if we could see each person as a masterpiece, created by God to be an essential part of his cosmic plan to renew, redeem, and restore all things? This verse provided the foundation for our leadership development: to look for beauty and giftedness in each person.[48]

What Miriam and Carlton are suggesting above is that the primary leadership team needs to create the connections and energy that allow the entire body to experience the joy of serving God together. This environment enables the community to behave as a coordinated maturing body, able to minister to its own internal needs even as it ministers to those beyond itself. The common vision they share for "every member a minister" is what pulls this together. Miriam describes this vision in terms of synergistic teams:

Synergistic teams demonstrate progress in developing

---

46 Ibid., 187.

47 Ibid., 186.

48 Carlton Deal, "Leadership and Organizational Development for Normal People," *Grow Where You're Planted*, Eds. Daniel Steigerwald and Kelly Crull (Portland: Christian Associates Press, 2013), 62, 65.

gifts because they are teams where a wide diversity of gifts are at work, but towards a shared goal. Each member has the humility to value everyone else's contribution and the boldness to step out and experiment with newly developing skills. Synergy happens when all team members reach their potential while experiencing the support of the team. Team members trust one another not only in relationship but also to do their part and carry their load in reaching the goal.[49]

Such teams, where each member's gifts are respected and empowered as all members of the team work toward a common goal, are an ideal sphere for discovering gifts and learning how to express them well. The primary leadership team will need to place a high priority on finding and developing gifted leaders to facilitate such teams. (In the next section, we'll provide exercises on how to do that).

As we seek to empower people, here's some time-tested advice: Investing in people, most of whom volunteer their time beyond their own demanding work/family schedules, requires that we *utilize them according to their calling and giftedness and not merely to fill empty positions we see as important!* This, of course, does not mean every act of service for the sake of the body must be along the lines of a person's gifts - owning our community means we all have our share in occasional "grunt work." But too often it's *only* the grunt work that leaders ask members of the body to carry out.

Discovering our Unique Design

So how do we help people express their unique role in the church? We need to address two other questions

first, as they will supply us with the information we need to answer this primary question. The first question is: *What are the individual's passions and gifts and how have those already begun to emerge in the community?* These can be discerned through a deliberate exploration of vocation that includes the use of interviews, diagnostic tools, and feedback. If the person has been serving in the community for some time already, the leadership team may find it helpful to conduct a 360 assessment using data from those working closely with the individual.

The second question we need to answer to get the information needed to empower people in their giftedness is often not as well explored as the first: *How does the individual live out their gifts in a way that is natural and satisfying to them?* God has uniquely designed every person, and that design is deeply satisfying to a person when it is able to be expressed. It's worth taking the time to explore how the passions, giftedness, and experience of each member fits with the church's vision and ministries - both present and potential. Further, attention should be given as to whether the member is gifted in ways primarily suited toward the inward focus of the church or its outward vision. Finding the right "fit" for each person allows them to flourish, resulting in wonderful blessing for the individual and also a win for the Kingdom!

The following series of exercises is designed to help your team explore the biblical concept of calling and apply it to your team context. They are also designed to equip your team to help members of the wider community discover their gifts and passions, so that they might find fulfilling ways to express them.

---

49 Miriam Phillips, "Releasing People into Their Divine Design," *Grow Where You're Planted*, 193.

Exploring the Apostle Paul's Use of CALLING

Time: 60-90 minutes
Supplies: Bibles, journal, copies of Appendix L, pens or pencils

1. Each person finds a discussion partner. With your partner pray and ask the Holy Spirit to guide you in this study session. Read texts that use a form of the Greek word, *kletos* (pronounced "klay-toss."): Matt. 22:14; Rom. 1:1, 6-7; 8:28; I Cor. 1:1-2, 24; Jude 1:1; Rev. 17:14 (available in Appendix L). After you read each passage aloud, cross out "calling" and write in "KLETOS" in each passage.

2. Reread each scripture passage studying the context. Discuss how you would translate, in your own words, the meaning of *kletos* each time it is used. To get a grasp of the meaning, make sure you consider the broader passage in which the word is used. Write down each of your translations next to each occurrence of *kletos*. Considering your translations of what *kletos* means in each passage, work with your partner to create your own definition of this word. (Hint: we are *kletos* (called) to "be" rather than to "do" - ministry flows out of who we are.)

3. Come together as a team to discuss each group's definitions. Respond to the following prompts:
    *   *How do your definitions differ from how churches typically use the word "calling?"*
    *   *How might your team incorporate a more accurate and fuller usage of this word so that volunteers might find a deeper fulfillment in their service to the Lord?*

4. Develop three guiding principles that will help your community activate their understanding of "calling/*kletos*." Record the guiding principles in your journal.

    Examples of guiding principles related to "*kletos*":
    *   *Our community will not press people into volunteer work just because we need someone to fill the position.*
    *   *We understand that we are all called to follow in the way of Jesus, not to a specific job in the organization. Therefore we will find a good fit for all positions within our community.*

Discerning the Unique Identity of Your Team Members

Time: Time depends on size of the group. Allow 30 minutes per person
Supplies: Writing paper, index cards, pens or pencils

We recommend this exercise be first practiced among your leadership team. Then, assemble the leaders of your ministry teams and small groups, and facilitate the exercise among them. Ideally, all leaders of your "synergistic teams" can then do the same exercise with their respective teams.

1. Start with prayer, asking God to guide the imagination of each person within the group. Provide 15 minutes of silence for the team. During this time each person reflects on a time when they felt fulfilled in what they were doing. (If this has never happened for them, maybe there is someone who they admire that they can use for this exercise - what is it that they do that I find so inspiring?).

2. Write this story of the event or activity on a sheet of paper, describing as much about it as possible. Note those activities or ways of being/leading/working, whichever applies, that are specifically fulfilling.

3. Take turns telling your stories of fulfillment. A person volunteers to tell their story to the team. When he/she is finished, the group will take one minute in silent prayer asking God to assist them in giving positive feedback about this person's gifts, as illustrated in their story or as they have observed the speaker. Persons in the group may ask clarifying questions.

4. Each group member will write the team member's name on the top of an index card, adding three or four thoughts or observations about the person's gifts, and then pass them to him/her. Team member reads aloud the input that they received for affirmation and appreciation. Facilitator affirms what has been shared.

5. Repeat until everyone has shared and received input.

Discovering Your Vocational Preferences

Time: 60 minutes
Supplies: Copies of Appendix M, cardstock, paper, markers of different colors, pens or pencils

As with the previous exercise, we recommend this exercise be first practiced among your leadership team. Ideally, all leaders of your "synergistic teams" can then do the same exercise with their respective teams. Finally, consider using this exercise with your small groups and other ministry teams. This exercise consists of two parts: Personal Reflection and Partner Discussion.

Personal Reflection:

1. Contemplate your work life, including paid jobs, volunteer jobs, and work that you have done within your family unit, noting each on a timeline. This can be a straight line, a spiral, or a circle. It might look like a mountain range or an ocean, or whatever pleases you. Add a visual representation of each job in your work life in chronological order, as noted above.

2. Near each job note your duties and the things for which you were responsible. Write the activities you did not enjoy below the line, and the activities you did enjoy above the line. Look for themes: What do you like to do and how? What is it about each particular job that you either liked or despised? Note your themes.

3. Go to Appendix M: Vocational Preferences and study each preference. Highlight three that seem most appealing to you. Compare those with what you observe in your work life. When you compare your work/job experience with the Vocational Preferences, what do you discover about yourself?

4. Now consider the feedback that you received in the previous learning exercise, ***Discerning the Unique Identity of Your Team Members***. How might these bits of self-knowledge help you to serve the Body of Christ more fully and authentically? What would you like to do to serve in your church or neighborhood?

Partner Discussion:

1. Find a discussion partner and explain to her what you have learned about yourself and how you would feel most authentic serving in the church or neighborhood. Explain to her what gifts and preferences support your desire.

2. Reverse roles and listen to your discussion partner as he explains what he has discovered about himself.

3. Take a few minutes to write a paragraph describing what your ideal work would be.

4. Listen as your discussion partner reads their paragraph, asking questions, and giving supportive input. Read your paragraph to your discussion partner. Discussion partner asks questions and gives supportive input.

Discovering the Gifts that Build Up the Body of Christ

Another aspect of the quest to release all members of the body of Christ in their unique calling, gift-edness, and experience is found in the Apostle Paul's instruction in chapter four of his letter to the Ephesians. Toward the middle of that chapter, in verses 7-13, Paul notes that God has given five primary gifts critical to the building up of the body of Christ – apostles, prophets, evangelists, shepherds, and teachers:

But to each one of us grace has been given as Christ apportioned it. This is why it says: "When he ascended on high, he took many captives and gave gifts to his people."...So Christ himself gave the apostles, the prophets, the evangelists, the pastors and teachers, to equip his people for works of service, so that the body of Christ may be built up until we all reach unity in the faith and in the knowledge of the Son of God and become mature, attaining to the whole measure of the fullness of Christ. - Eph. 4:7-8,11-13

Notice first of all, in verse seven, these gifts ("graces" literally) have been apportioned among the entire body – "to each one of us" - not only among those who are leader-gifted. Secondly, they are given in their full five-fold range for the equipping of the church, so that it might mature to the "whole measure of the fullness of Christ." In other words, *we need all of these gifts to see local bodies rise to the full stature of Christ.*

We have discovered that understanding these gifts in our own lives can help us develop and use them so that they edify and equip the church. The following definitions developed by Alan Hirsch provide perspective on how these gifts operate in community.

APOSTLES extend the gospel. As the "sent ones," they ensure that the faith is transmitted from one context to another and from one generation to the next. They are always thinking about the future, bridging barriers, establishing the church in new contexts, developing leaders, and networking trans-locally. Yes, if you focus solely on initiating new ideas and rapid expansion, you can leave people and organizations wounded. The shepherding and teaching functions are needed to ensure people are cared for rather than simply used.

PROPHETS know God's will. They are particularly attuned to God and his truth for today. They bring correction and challenge the dominant assumptions we inherit from the culture. They insist that the community obey what God has commanded. They question the status quo. Without the other types of leaders in place, prophets can become belligerent activists or, paradoxically, disengage from the imperfection of reality and become other-worldly.

EVANGELISTS recruit. These infectious communicators of the gospel message recruit others to the cause. They call for a personal response to God's redemption in Christ, and also draw believers to engage the wider mission, growing the church. Evangelists can be so focused on reaching those outside the church that maturing and strengthening those inside is neglected.

SHEPHERDS nurture and protect. Caregivers of the community, they focus on the protection and spiritual maturity of God's flock, cultivating a loving and spiritually mature network of relationships, making and developing disciples. Shepherds can value stability to the detriment of the mission. They may also foster an unhealthy dependence between the church and themselves.

Dynamic Adventure

TEACHERS understand and explain. Communicators of God's truth and wisdom, they help others remain biblically grounded to better discern God's will, guiding others toward wisdom, helping the community remain faithful to Christ's word, and constructing a transferable doctrine. Without the input of the other functions, teachers can fall into dogmatism or dry intellectualism. They may fail to see the personal or missional aspects of the church's ministry.[50]

Because the APEST gifts are such an important aspect of a local church's *maturing*, we provide the following exercises to help your community understand and activate them.

---

50 Alan Hirsch, "What is APEST?" http://www.theforgotten-ways.org/apest/ (accessed 11 May 2016).

Discovering Your APEST Gifts

Time: 90 minutes
Supplies: Bible, five large sheets of paper, markers, pens or pencils

1. Each team member reads Alan Hirsch's APEST descriptions above, underlining words or phrases that seem significant. Circle the top two descriptions that most accurately describe you.

2. Volunteer reads aloud Ephesians 4:1-16. Pay special attention to the five-fold APEST gifts in verse 11.

3. Post five large sheets of paper on the wall around the room, each with a different APEST gift written at the top. Participants move around the room visiting each sheet, adding their own action words, phrases, or images that describe that gift.

4. Five volunteers, one for each APEST gift, read to the group the collective descriptions of each gift. Facilitator leads discussion inviting any remaining questions about the gifts, adding clarifying words or phrases to the sheets as needed.

5. Each member of the team revisits each of the five sheets, reading the descriptors and images for each gift, prayerfully considering how well each gift describes her. After considering all five gifts, she signs her name at the bottom of the two sheets representing the APEST gifts that best describe her, circling her name on the sheet she feels represents her most prominent gift.

6. Gathered as a team, members take turns sharing their gifting, how the images or descriptors resonate with them, and how they may have seen their selected gifts operative in their lives. After each person shares, the facilitator leads a brief discussion allowing other team members to comment on and affirm the speaker's gifting. Team members record their APEST gifts in their journals along with any helpful descriptors or images. Facilitator retains the five APEST sheets for use in subsequent exercises.

Creating an Atmosphere of APEST Collaboration in Leadership

Time: 90 minutes

*Supplies: Paper, whiteboard and markers, APEST gift sheets from the **Discovering Your APEST Gifts** learning exercise, pens or pencils*

1. As a team, consider a key ministry question that you now face. Facilitator writes the question on the whiteboard. Examples: How do we include our non-Christian friends in our community? Should we hold a weekly Sunday gathering? Is it time rent a facility?

2. Gather into five groups according to your top APEST gifting. Distribute the APEST gift sheets to their respective groups. Each group reviews the words and images on their APEST gift sheet and then develops a response to the question on the whiteboard from the vantage point of their APEST gift.

3. When prompted, each group presents their response to the team.

4. After all groups have shared, discuss the following as a team:
    *   *What similarities are there in our groups' responses? What differences are there?*
    *   *How do the differences in our perspectives affect potential solutions to the ministry question in view?*
    *   *What steps can we take to ensure that all five APEST perspectives are integrated into our decision making process? Examples: Invite those outside leadership who have clear gifts in other APEST areas to speak into decisions. Ask team members to put on their respective APEST "hat" during one phase of discernment. Gather into groups according to APEST gifts during our decision making process to more fully develop and compare each APEST perspective on an issue.*

Bringing APEST Balance to Your Team

Time: 90 minutes

*Supplies: APEST gift sheets from the **Discovering Your APEST Gifts** learning exercise, copies of Appendix N, pens or pencils*

1. Each team member reads the selection from *The Permanent Revolution* in Appendix N, underlining anything that seems significant.

2. Gathered as a team, take turns sharing your underlines. Discuss words or phrases in the passage that seem important. Facilitator notes them on the whiteboard.

3. Gather into five groups according to your top APEST gifting. Distribute the APEST gift sheets to their respective groups. Look around the room at the five groups. Which giftings are underrepresented on your team? Which are overrepresented?

4. Using the descriptors and images on the gift sheets along with the reading selection from *The Permanent Revolution*, discuss in your group the potential dangers associated with the under or overrepresentation of your group's gifting on the team. List a few simple steps you might take to lessen that danger.

5. Come together as a team. Groups take turns sharing their responses. After all groups have shared, use the following questions to discuss what you have learned about the gift mix of your team:
   - *How equally are the APEST gifts represented on our team?*
   - *Which gifts are under or overrepresented on our team and what potential strengths and dangers does that pose?*
   - *If there is substantial imbalance of gifting on our team, what are two or three actions we can take to promote balance on our team? Examples: Incorporate APEST perspectives into our decision-making process. Invite a volunteer to become an APEST expert to help us better understand our team dynamics. Consider a person's APEST gifting when we are recruiting a new team member.*

Developing the Depth and Capacity of the Church's Leadership Community

In this section we address the issue of leadership in the church. We discuss what leading and the gift of leadership are, as well as consider how to identify and develop leaders. Finally, we introduce how to implement leadership structures for the church to continue its *maturing* for years to come.

Exploring Leadership

Before digging into this subject, we want to acknowledge that the word "leadership" may have quite a range of meaning from one person to the next on your team or in your faith community. We also realize that for some people it may bring to mind memories of hurtful experiences. With these possibilities in mind, we provide two exercises from the outset to help you be less encumbered in your practice of leadership together.

This first exercise is designed both to stimulate learning among your team about the subject of leadership, and also to help you arrive at a working definition of the word "leadership" itself.

Exploring the Meaning of Leadership

Time: 2 hours plus time to read a book, read blogs, or watch a movie
Supplies: Copies of Appendix O, whiteboard and markers

1. Each team member chooses a different book to read on leadership (see the Appendix O: Leadership Books for ideas, but feel free to develop a list appropriate to your setting). If reading books is not appealing to you, then figure out a way to explore leadership through other means. For example: read leadership blogs, interview exemplary leaders using "Open Questions," watch and take notes on movies such as *Invictus, Calgary,* or *The Mission*, etc.

2. Prepare a brief review of your book, movie, blog, etc., highlighting the most important elements, including the author's definition of leadership. Each person brings their findings on leadership via a bullet pointed presentation to the group. The facilitator records on the whiteboard keywords or phrases that come up in the presentations. The group asks the presenter clarifying questions if needed.

3. Once every person has presented, the group compares and contrasts the ideas that have been presented, looking for similarities and differences. Use the following prompts to aid your discussion:
   - *What are the two most helpful ideas or insights that we might put into practice?*
   - *Which ideas do not apply to our situation?*
   - *What further questions do we have?*

4. Using the information gleaned in step three, the facilitator guides the group in formulating a short working definition of leadership (no longer than one paragraph) that is agreeable to the team.

This next exercise is designed to help individual team members process hurtful or negative experiences related to people in authority. If you have been hurt by a leader, or if you have struggled with the concept of leadership because of bad examples, then the following reflective exercise is for you. Be aware, however, this exercise might unearth emotions that may require you to seek outside counsel to work through.

Moving Beyond Cynicism or Hurt Related to Leaders

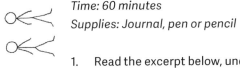

Time: 60 minutes
Supplies: Journal, pen or pencil

1. Read the excerpt below, underlining ideas that catch your interest in any way.

    Many have been hurt or disillusioned by poor leadership, and some by leadership that could even rightly be called sinful. Stories abound of Christian leaders who have succumbed to pride, lust for power, sexual temptation, financial impropriety, narcissism – name your poison.

    Far too many people have experienced a domineering kind of leader – a person who quenched their voice, or who limited their influence. We think in particular of how hard it often is for women in the church, or for those who are not white males. Many women and men, for various reasons, carry hurt or resentment from those who have led them poorly, or who have taken advantage of them in the past.

    Perhaps you have been hurt or angered by your experience of leadership in the past. God wants to help you through that, to give you God's perspective on leadership as it is intended to be practiced in the church – keeping in mind that leaders are fallen people too. We acknowledge your pain, and we hope that the Communitas community and its way of living out leadership can be healing to your soul. We invite you to speak up, bring it to our attention if you notice or experience inequities.

    The author of Hebrews offers the body of Christ this gentle nudge: "Have confidence in your leaders and submit to their authority, because they keep watch over you as those who must give an account. Do this so that their work will be a joy, not a burden, for that would be of no benefit to you." - Hebrews 13:17

    God desires that you trust and respect those called to lead you. This may require forgiveness on your part. But you also may have to take responsibility for behavior and certain attitudes that unnecessarily burden those placed in your life as leaders. None of us wants to be responsible for sapping joy from our leaders, or somehow eroding their effectiveness in growing the church. And where we carry unresolved issues from the past, it inevitably bleeds out in our own leadership and negatively affects those we lead.[51]

2. Share what you underlined with your mentor and tell why it was important to you. If this text creates tension or resistance in your soul, pause now and acknowledge your emotions in writing.

3. Prayerfully ask God to shed light on why you feel the way you do. Ask God to guide you toward healing. Journal what you hear the Holy Spirit telling you.

---

51   Excerpted from material prepared by Dan Steigerwald in September, 2011 for Communitas' online "Matrix" training.

4. Make a plan to talk to someone about your pain. You may decide to see a therapist. Find a prayer partner to support you in your process. Create an accountability plan with your mentor for working through your tension, pain, and/or resistance.

It's helpful to get a big-picture perspective on leadership. We trust that if necessary you've begun to address the pain of past experiences that makes it hard to believe leadership can be exercised in healthy ways. We now want to turn our attention to leadership in the body of Christ. As you'll soon note below, we in Communitas believe that anyone can exercise leadership. At the same time, we also believe that leadership is a spiritual gift God gives to certain people to aid the development of the body of Christ.

In Romans 12 the Apostle Paul suggests that leadership is a God-given gift:

6 "We have different gifts, according to the grace given to each of us. If your gift is prophesying, then prophesy in accordance with your faith; 7 if it is serving, then serve; if it is teaching, then teach; 8 if it is to encourage, then give encouragement; if it is giving, then give generously; if it is to lead, do it diligently; if it is to show mercy, do it cheerfully." - Romans 12:6-8

In the above passage to *lead diligently* translates two Greek words. W.E. Vine and Colin Brown explain these words meant an ability or calling to stand before others, "providing care, direction, protection and support" in the first century.[52] From Vine and Brown we could conclude that a spiritual gift of leadership involves *an ability or calling to go before others with a heart that seeks the welfare of the community, representing its values and facilitating its growth and development.*

In the Bible the Apostle Paul is not the only one who draws our attention to this special capacity to lead God's people. We see leadership displayed throughout the entire narrative of Scripture. In the Old Testament we see leadership exercised by the patriarchs, by judges, prophets, priests, and kings, as well as military men. We see God using both men and women in major national oversight functions, as with Joseph, Deborah, Daniel, Esther, Nehemiah, and others. In the long narrative of Israel's history, we see many examples of bad leadership that are counterbalanced by quite a few stories of good leadership.

In the New Testament we see the birth of the body of Christ, the Church, under the headship or leadership of Jesus. And, over time, we see the emergence of many local groups of believers, with specific leaders called and chosen to steward their development in the various towns and cities across the Roman empire. The testimony of "Christians" (Acts 11:26) across the Roman empire is that the resurrected Jesus is truly Lord - supreme Leader - not Caesar or any other power. And those overseeing local churches are called upon to assist their "flocks" in following this King, so that no individual leader or church exists apart from their subjection to Jesus' leadership. This fundamental reality of Jesus as supreme Leader above all ought to inform every aspect of the way we understand and conduct leadership as Christians.

Looking further into the New Testament, we see a pattern emerge for local church leadership that involved the empowering of overseers or "elders." This form of leadership draws from the Jewish

---

52 Richard Rardin, *The Servant's Guide to Leadership* (Canada: Selah Publishing, 2001), 40-41.

model, where wise and experienced men oversaw the political and religious affairs of Israel (e.g. In the New Testament era such elders were leaders of the Jewish synagogue). All New Testament churches seem to have adopted this pattern and were overseen or shepherded by a designated team of elders.[53] For example, in Acts 14:23 we read:

"Paul and Barnabas appointed elders for them in each church and, with prayer and fasting, committed them to the Lord, in whom they had put their trust."

Note that Paul and Barnabas appointed elders in *each* church. These elders operated as a plurality of equals, but also seemed to characteristically appoint a point leader who was "first among equals" (e.g. James, who stood prominent as the point leader at Jerusalem). In Communitas we endorse point leadership always within the framework of shared leadership, and we allow each team to determine how it will structure its long-term leadership team. Shared configurations, under whatever structure a team or church chooses, allow the expression of a diversity of leadership orientations (Eph. 4:11). They also provide a safeguard to protect leaders from behaviors that might be destructive to them and to those they lead.

The Bible suggests that God gifts certain individuals with the capacity to lead others. This gift, like the many other gifts God bestows, is needed to enable the body of Christ to flourish. It is a particularly important gift as leaders provide much of the primary energy and abilities needed to move groups toward their God-sized dreams.

Identifying and Developing Leaders

As we use this term "leadership" in the *maturing* of faith communities, we distinguish between what it means to exercise leadership and what it means to function as a leader. Many argue that leadership at its most basic level is simply influence, and we tend to agree. Dr. J. Robert Clinton would argue that anyone in the body of Christ can exert leadership, because any person can engage in what he calls a "leadership act." A leadership act, as Clinton sees it, "occurs when a given person influences a group, in terms of behavioral acts or perception, so that the group acts or thinks differently."[54]

A leadership act has the following four components:

1. An **influencer** – this may be one of several persons.
2. The **followers** – person or persons who are being influenced.
3. **Influence** – the behavior and perception that brings about change.
4. A **change** – the different way of perceiving and behaving by the group.

Any person in the body of Christ can engage in these acts because we all have the capacity, in a given moment, to influence others. Such acts occur around us every day. In the home setting, different family members influence the behavior or actions of the family. In the workplace, influence and leadership acts occur whether or not the individuals have a formed leadership position or responsibility. In the local church, different members exercise acts of influence, as they knowingly, or unknowingly, influence those within the church to behave or perceive

---

53 Alexander Strauch, *Biblical Eldership: An Urgent Call to Restore Biblical Church Leadership* (Littleton: Lewis & Roth, 1995), 121-124.

54 J. Robert Clinton, *Leadership Emergence Theory* (Altadena: Barnabas Resources, 1989), 34.

issues in a particular way.[55]

According to Clinton, just because a person engages in various leadership acts, it doesn't mean that person is a "leader." Only those who *frequently* and *persistently* engage in the act of leadership (influence) can be classified as leaders. In other words, in contrast to those who perform isolated or occasional leadership acts, a leader is one who *consistently* performs leadership acts that support God's purposes for the group. Therefore, to determine those that are leaders, we need to ask such questions as:

- Who is consistently helping the group move forward toward their preferred future (vision)?
- Who is consistently inspiring and mobilizing people to live in ways consistent with the values of the group?
- Who is consistently creating or stewarding momentum that leads to growth of the community, both qualitatively and quantitatively?
- Who is consistently helping the group to respond in a timely manner to needs and God-given opportunities?

These are the kind of repetitive acts we commonly find among those who are leader-gifted.

Frequency of leadership influence, as expressed through the actions noted above, is one of the stronger markers for identifying those gifted to lead. But there are other helpful markers. Clinton commonly uses the acronym "F.A.T." to highlight the three additional characteristics he sees as crucial to the identifying and selecting of leaders:

1. Faithfulness
2. Availability
3. Teachableness[56]

Therefore we must also ask when considering leaders:

- Who do we observe that is faithful, or who is it that consistently engages what they sense God and others are asking of them?
- Who do we see that is also able to make the time to learn and do what needs to be done?
- And who, in addition to possessing these traits, also demonstrates a learning posture, not proud or overly confident in their capacities but ever open to learn and discover where grace, skill, and wisdom can unite for advantage to the Kingdom?

In God's way of doing things, of course, we see that giftedness to lead is only one aspect of good leadership. The quality and character of leaders is affirmed by Scripture as even weightier criteria than being able to lead and equip groups to achieve their vision. Those researching many thousands of leaders (e.g. Kouzes and Posner, J. Robert Clinton, Max DePree, etc.) are unified in affirming that the character of the leader and the manner in which leaders lead are even more important than the exercise of competencies that move communities forward.

Good leadership as we see it involves using power, position, and influence in ways that honor Christ and place Him and the interests of the group above our own agendas. Another way to say this is: Godly leaders perform consistent acts of servanthood,

---

55 Ibid., 34-36, with some reworking by Dr. Paul Leavenworth of Convergence Group (www.theconvergencegroup.org).

56 Brian Newman, formerly Communitas' Europe Director, popularized this F.A.T. criteria in Communitas, which he gleaned from his mentor, Dr. J. Robert Clinton, who authored *The Making of a Leader* (Colorado Springs: Navpress, 1988).

compassion, and discernment for the good of the group and the glory of God. They build up those under their care (Ephesians 4:11-16), and they influence God's people to love and serve Christ more deeply and passionately.

In Communitas' ranks, we have been graced with many such leaders - both female and male - beginning with our founder, Linus Morris. Dr. Wesley White, who we referred to earlier in this chapter, and his wife Cindy are an example of humble, Jesus-honoring leadership. Mike Kurtyka, who has served alongside them for more than a decade, offers this:

I have seen servant leadership modelled by Wes & Cindy White over our many years ministering together in Glasgow Mosaic and now in a new project, Upper Room Church. While hospitality is something our families value and we all open our homes regularly, they have a unique ability to love others.

Our Iranian brothers and sisters who make up the core of Upper Room have embraced faith in Jesus, Christian community, and serving one another, because Wes & Cindy loved them well as they plainly demonstrated these things. Imagine 50-60 people coming every Friday into a three bedroom (European sized) flat to have a meal, sing songs, study God's

Word, and to pray. It's no small feat, and often Wes & Cindy stay up late cleaning, and arise early, to finish the tidying up (not to mention their son Aiden's involvement). Recently, Wes visited a member of Upper Room who had just returned from the hospital. Brother M surprised Wes by asking for Bibles for Upper Room on Wednesday. Wes gently corrected Brother M that he meant Friday. Insisting it was Wednesday, Brother M showed him a photo from his phone of ten people gathered in his flat for an Upper Room that he had started on Wednesdays. Truly sacrificial servant leadership was being replicated as Brother M lives on $50/week!

I am privileged and humbled to witness their servant leadership flowing from their contagious love for Christ. There is power in the name of Jesus and they are giving testimony to His name by serving and loving well.

Communitas makes it a priority to identify, train, empower, and support leader-gifted individuals so that they might rise to this quality of character. Wes and Cindy, like any of us, have their day to day struggles and are not perfect. But the quest to remain authentic and *maturing* as people is one worth pursuing.

The following exercise will help you imagine the characteristics of a leader worth following.

Describing the Kind of Leaders We're Glad to Follow

Time: 75 minutes
Supplies: Large sheets of paper, markers

1. With a discussion partner, review Clinton's distinction between those who perform occasional leadership acts and those who do so consistently. How are the two different? Name the differences that you observe.

2. Name three or four of the most gifted leaders that you have known. What characteristics do you notice, both positive and negative, in their lives? What do you suppose their values were? Name two or three.

3. On a large sheet of paper with your partner draw a life-size symbol of a leader (you might want to trace his or her outline on the paper). Inside your symbol write the values that you would find important in a leader that you would feel confident working with. Include the character traits that you named in step two.

4. Gather as a team. Each pair shares their image and values with the entire team. After every pair has shared, facilitator leads the team to create a collection of character traits and values of the ideal leader.

It's good to have an image of the ideal leader that we can all aspire to. In reality, however, no such person exists - only those growing toward the ideal. Growing as a leader is a continuous, lifelong process. And, as mentioned earlier in this chapter, growth is best accomplished through deliberate action surrounded by supportive relationship.

Therefore, as you identify and raise up potential leaders, you will need to be intentional about developing their leadership abilities. Developing leaders is a conscious investment of your time and energy within your unique situation, allowing context and culture to contour the process. Leadership development can occur in informal "teach-as-you-go" environments or through formal programs. Reading a book together, starting a group to study leadership under Christ, providing opportunities to shadow existing leaders, or leading a small group could all be means to develop leaders. We encourage you to search out and use a method that is suited to your context and people. Al Dyck tells of a leadership development program he recently employed in Madrid, Spain:

In a church full of people 20 years younger than I, I recognized the need for leadership development. As I looked around me, I saw young people leading small groups, leading ministries to the homeless, leading worship, but with few

mentors around to build into them. I decided to develop a six-month course called In Step Leader Development *that would help them intentionally engage their own growth as leaders.*

Gabriella was one of the young leaders who I invited to participate in the first course. Active in our homeless ministry, she came to the course eager to learn. Every two weeks she and a small group of other leaders would meet for two hours examining their stories, values, strengths, and gifts as leaders. Through Bible study and outside reading, we gained a strong biblical foundation for leadership. Gabriella went on to lead the homeless outreach ministry and help me facilitate the next course for a new group of leaders.

A large variety of resources is available to help your team gain insights, frameworks, and models for leadership development. Your leadership study from the learning exercise **Exploring the Meaning of Leadership** is a good place to start. For further exploration, Communitas offers a comprehensive leadership development track via its FUEL learning cohort. The Forge Mission Training Network offers a missional leadership module as part of its training. Still other recommendations include *The Leadership Challenge* by Kouzes and Posner, *In the Name of Jesus* by Henri Nouwen, and The Situational Leadership Model as developed by Ken Blanchard, et al.

Dynamic Adventure

Finally, it bears repeating that any leadership development plan needs to be tailored to the unique requirements of the people in your context. There is no one-size-fits-all method to develop the individuals God has given you. The following questions are offered to help you formulate a leadership development plan that is right for you and your team:

- Will our development process be more informal "teach-as-you-go" or programmatic?
- What curriculum or materials will we use to develop both the competency and character of our potential leaders?
- Will the development process take place as a group or one-on-one with each person?
- What are we inviting each person to do, and how will we communicate that to them?
- What commitment are we asking for from each potential leader?
- What, if anything, do we expect from the potential leaders after their development?
- Who from our team will be responsible for each potential leader?

Implementing Appropriate Leadership Structures

In addition to identifying and developing leaders, it is critical for every maturing church to set in place a leadership structure to oversee the governance of the body. As Carlton Deal, founding pastor of The Well in Brussels, Belgium, puts it: "A maturing missional church is one that has carefully thought through its leadership structure and is implementing a Biblically-based and culturally-relevant leadership model. Europe needs more of these kinds of churches."[57]

On the road to church planting, leaders will eventually encounter this need to develop a more permanent leadership structure or "polity" for their forming communities. Remko Dekker, one of the founders of Crossroads Leiden, shares how his leadership team has recently come to this point in their own journey:

For Crossroads Leiden, we are convinced that our next steps in maturing include figuring out how to empower longer-term senior leadership to carry the church into the next season of development. We strongly feel that we need gifted individuals to "equip the saints for ministry" over the longer haul. From the beginning we have included people in our decision-making and activities, and we have invited them into ownership of the church's development. We have noticed that when people own and embrace the vision and who we want to be as a people (our identity), the more we collectively give away ministry and the more we ourselves are ministered to. This "giving away" starts small (as do most projects), and it grows as we discover the giftings, competence, and character in the people God brings us. We have moved from giving away tasks, however, to giving away ministries. And now we are in the process of giving away the project!

For us this [empowering of longer-term leadership] means inviting people to participate on an elder board that has final authority in leadership matters for the church. These elders can move the church beyond its founding leaders, and help it discern its own sense of what the church needs for the future. We feel an elder-led model offers the necessary checks and balances that are a good path towards a healthy self-sustaining community. And we are particularly happy to see women leaders step up to take their place! In our experience a mixed team is stronger and wiser; and it is a better reflection of who the community desires to be.

---

57 Carlton Deal, "Leadership and Organizational Development for Normal People," *Grow Where You're Planted*, 61.

Remko and his leadership team are presently working to develop an elder-type polity or structure to serve and sustain their church into the future. In Communitas' experience many new or forming churches choose an elder-based structure of church leadership, as that seems to be most consistent with New Testament teaching.

As Remko's story suggests above, we recommend a slow and deliberate approach to developing a church governing structure. Decisions on leadership structures will have long-term (positive or negative) impact on the future health and sustainability of a faith community. The following learning exercises are meant to help your team examine Scripture to understand the functions and qualifications of "elders" or "overseers" in the church.

Discovering the Functions of Overseers in the Church

Time: 90 minutes
Supplies: Bibles, whiteboard and markers, sticky-notes, pens or pencils

1. In groups of four or less, review the following scripture texts that describe the *functions* that primary leaders were called to exercise in serving local churches: I Tim. 5:17; I Pet. 5:2-3; Acts 15:28; James 5:14; Acts 20:28-31; Heb. 13:7, 17. As you read each text, note the function or role church leaders are called to fill.

2. List each function on a sticky-note. Use a single word or phrase to describe each function, then write a brief sentence or two describing what you think it means.

3. Discuss in your groups: Which functions do you have questions about? Are there other functions you would add (and if so, what Bible texts call for that particular function)?

4. Come together as a team. Groups take turns sharing their noted functions, posting each sticky-note on the whiteboard, and reading their definition aloud. After groups share, the facilitator arranges the sticky-notes according to similarity of function.

5. When all groups have shared their notes, facilitator leads the team to discuss teammates' questions regarding any of the functions and then to develop a short definition for each function. Facilitator writes each definition on the whiteboard. Record the functions and definitions in your journal. Facilitator records these for future reference.

Examining the Qualifications for Overseers in the Church

Time: 90 minutes
Supplies: Bibles, whiteboard and markers, sticky-notes, pens or pencils

1. In groups of four or less, review the following scripture texts highlighting the *qualifications* of overseers in the church: I Tim. 3:2-7; Titus 1:6-9; I Peter 5:1-4. As you read each text, note the qualifications of church leaders.

2. List each qualification on a sticky-note. Use a single word or phrase to describe each qualification, then write a brief sentence or two describing what you think it means.

3. Discuss in your groups: Which qualifications do you have questions about? Are there other qualifications you would add (and if so, what Bible texts call for that particular qualification)?

4. Come together as a team. Groups take turns sharing their noted qualifications, posting each sticky-note on the whiteboard, and reading their definition aloud. As groups share, the facilitator arranges the sticky-notes according to similarity of qualification.

5. When all groups have shared their notes, facilitator leads the team to discuss teammates' questions regarding any of the qualification and then to develop a short definition for each qualification. Facilitator writes each definition on the whiteboard. Record the qualification and definitions in your journal. Facilitator records these for future reference.

As you can see from the above exercises, the qualifications for and responsibilities of elders are substantial. Appointing one or more people to the role of overseer or elder has long-term consequences for the local church. Selecting the right person(s) for the role is important. We strongly suggest that you work with a mature coach or mentor during the initial process of selecting candidates.

The following exercise is intended to spark your imagination to think creatively about potential overseers in your church. Each individual on your leadership team can take the exercise to a trusted mentor, using it to process through the team's work on the functions and qualifications of overseers. This will provide external and wise input on initial thoughts of who could fill these important roles. However, the eventual selection of overseers will be part of a longer term process we discuss below.

Stirring Your Imagination for Potential Overseers in the Church

Time: 2 hours
Supplies: Journal, paper, pen or pencil, documents containing outcomes of learning exercises:
Discovering the Functions of Overseers in the Church *and* **Examining the Qualifications for Overseers in the Church**

1. Review the team's work on leadership functions from the previous learning exercise, **Discovering the Functions of Overseers in the Church**. Describe each function to your mentor. What questions do you have about any of the functions? Discuss them with your mentor. List in your journal the five functions that are most essential to your church in its current season.

2. Review the list of overseer qualifications from the previous exercise, **Examining the Qualifications for Overseers in the Church**. Describe each qualification to your mentor. What questions do you have about any of the qualifications? Discuss them with your mentor.

3. Consider who in your community has these qualifications and is already influencing others along the lines of the prioritized leadership functions in step one. Make a list of suitable candidates (consider their APEST gifting!). Tell your mentor why you have selected them. Share with your mentor any questions or concerns you may have about any of the candidates.

4. Commit to a season of prayer for the candidates and for continued discernment moving forward.

While the above exercises provide an important foundation for understanding leadership structures, the actual work of developing them is more involved and beyond the scope of this workbook. We recommend you form a working group to study and direct leadership structure decisions. This working group should conduct an in-depth study of church polity and guide the practical work of developing leadership structures and of deciding how to select and approve overseers.

A good first step for your working group would be to read and discuss together a book such as *Eldership and the Mission of God*, by J.R. Briggs and Bob

Hyatt. Or to gain insight into governing structures other than a "plurality of elders," we recommend *Perspectives on Church Government*, by Chad Owen Brand and R. Stanton Norman. These and similar books will help deepen your collective understanding of various governance models in order to formulate the structure that is appropriate for your church in your unique context.

Further down the road your working group, along with members of the wider faith community, will need to solidify a set of principles by which your "overseers" or "elders" govern the body. Together, you will likely need to wrestle with questions such as:

- What type of governing model do we wish to adopt?
- Will we form an "elder board?" Something else? What is their role and scope of authority in the church?
- How many elders or overseers should we have in our church or project?
- How will we as a leadership team and church select and then approve candidates for elder or overseer?
- How long will an elder or overseer serve? Is appointment to elder or overseer a lifetime commitment or for a limited term?
- How frequently should our elders or overseers meet and for what purpose?
- How would we remove an elder or overseer, and what are the conditions that would make it necessary to do so?

Discerning Appropriate Progress Targets For the Season at Hand

Throughout this chapter we've presented some elements that are key to the *maturing* of any local body of Christ: affirming vision, empowering the body, and developing leadership depth and capacity. We've selected these in particular because we find that they are common starting places for any faith community desiring to grow up. You may have noticed, however, that we have been careful to avoid prescribing what any given church's journey of *maturing* ought to look like. Yet the question remains, how do we know that as a *maturing* church we are "headed in the right direction," that our community is making wise decisions presently, and sensible plans for our future?

Over many years of observing churches as they move from *embedding* and *initiating* through to *practicing* and *maturing*, we have noticed a number of characteristics that seem to be critical to the *maturing* of any local church. In Communitas we call these characteristics the "hallmarks of maturing church."[58] Through our study of Scripture and of the church, historically and in our present era, we have identified twelve such hallmarks. We don't suggest that twelve is some perfect number or that our list is complete. Nor do we attempt to rank any given hallmark by importance. This collection of hallmarks is simply *one* means by which churches might become more deliberate about discerning progress targets appropriate to their unique circumstances and stage of development.

We invite you to view the hallmarks as "dashboard" items, not twelve more demands placed upon your team. They are like the gauges and lights on the instrument panel of your car. It's wise to pay attention to your speed, fuel gauge, engine temperature, and especially those "need maintenance" lights! But you don't want to spend too much time looking down at the dashboard. Your job as a team is to keep your eyes looking ahead through the windshield, fixed on the road and moving toward your destination. Keep the focus on your community's vision, and pause occasionally to check on the needs of your "vehicle." Don't spend too much time looking at the dashboard or you may well run off the road!

---

58 A hallmark is defined as "a distinguishing characteristic, trait or feature." Miriam Webster Dictionary, http://mw4.merriam-webster.com/wdictionary/hallmark (Accessed 27 March 2015). After years of processing with hundreds of planters and church leaders, Communitas arrived at our twelve hallmarks and produced the book that we've already referenced called *Grow Where You're Planted!* Through real life stories of communities living into each hallmark, the book shows the meaning and value of these as discernment markers to help teams set growth targets.

The exercises that follow are designed to help your team interact with the twelve hallmarks to get a big-picture view of the many facets of *maturing*. They are tools to help you discern for yourselves what hallmarks you want to use to help *mature* your unique community. The second exercise will help your team explore how to integrate one of the hallmarks into your team planning and goal setting. We want you to practice this because we find that when teams set their own goals for growth, they usually achieve them!

Understanding and Prioritizing the Hallmarks of Maturing Church

Time: 90 minutes
Supplies: Copies of Appendix P, pens or pencils

1. With a discussion partner, review the hallmarks and their descriptions in Appendix P. After you have reviewed them, discuss these questions:
   - *What needs clarifying?*
   - *What is missing?*
   - *What questions do I have?*
   Note in your journal what you do not understand.

2. Add any missing elements to your list of hallmarks. Evaluate where your community stands with each of the hallmarks. Write a number from "1" to "10" in the margin next to each hallmark, with ten being "we've got this one" and one being "we need a lot of help."

3. Review with your discussion partner how you scored the list of hallmarks in light of where you sense God is leading your community overall. Circle the two hallmarks that you feel are most important for your community's development in this season.

4. Make a date with your mentor or leader to discuss missing elements or those you don't understand.

We find that at any given season perhaps only one to three of the hallmarks are "live issues" for a group or church. Which ones are relevant will depend on such factors as the group's unique size, setting, vision, resources, and stage of development. The following exercise is designed to help your team discern which hallmarks might be most relevant for you, while also encouraging you to set goals that allow your community to make progress where it counts the most. If you have a larger leadership team, you may be able to implement action plans for three to four hallmarks at the same time. However, the norm would be to focus on your top two most important hallmarks.

Using the Hallmarks to Set Progress Targets

Time: 90 minutes, plus time to implement plans in context
*Supplies: Copies Appendix P, completed work from previous exercise **Understanding and Prioritizing the Hallmarks of Maturing Church**, whiteboard and markers, large sheets of paper, markers, pens or pencils*

1. Each team member presents the two hallmarks he or she felt were the most important for the church's development from the exercise **Understanding and Prioritizing the Hallmarks of Maturing Church** above. The team discusses each suggestion, noting them on the whiteboard, and decides upon the two hallmarks that they will prioritize for the community. Collectively review the descriptions of the two hallmarks you've decided on, read the supporting Scripture references, and highlight that which seems most important to you.

2. In small groups of four or less. Each group receives a large sheet of paper and markers. Discuss the selected two hallmarks using these questions for evaluation:
   - *What is at stake if we fail to take action on these hallmarks?*
   - *What do we dream of doing that will help our community grow to maturity for these hallmarks?*
   On the large sheet of paper, make a list of your top three or four actions for each hallmark.

3. Discuss in your small groups: If we had $1000 to spend on implementing our actions for each hallmark, how would we divide up that money? Write specific amounts next to each action you listed above, keeping in mind that the total investment must not exceed $1000.

4. Gather as a team for discussion. Each group posts their paper on the wall and then presents their proposals on how the $1000 should be spent on actions for each hallmark. After all groups have shared, the facilitator leads the team to review together the spending proposals. Use the following prompts to start the discussion:
   - *Where is there agreement on priorities? Where are there differences?*
   - *Where is there similarity between our actions? Where are there differences?*
   - *Where are the individual spending proposals similar? Where are they different?*

5. Facilitator continues the discussion by asking the following question:

   After considering all these actions and spending proposals, if we actually had $1000 to spend on each hallmark, what three actions would we take for each?

   Allow time for the team to discuss and negotiate. Record the final proposals - actions and spending amounts - for each hallmark on a sheet of large paper. Retain this final draft. It contains significant insight into progress targets for your faith community. You may wish to continue work on these proposals in future team meetings, even implement them if finances allow. See the following additional steps below:

Optional next steps:

1. Facilitator leads the team to review the proposals for growth in each of your team's selected hallmarks as drafted in the exercise: **Using the Hallmarks to Set Progress Targets**. Are the growth goals, actions, and spending targets still appropriate? Update them as necessary.

2. Discuss the financial viability of implementing one or both of the proposals:
    *   *Are funds available for one or both of the proposals?*
    *   *If not, will we raise the funds we need? How?*
    *   *Based on finances available, which proposal will we implement first?*

3. Invite members of the team to be the "champion" responsible for each action in the proposal (Note: there should be three actions for each hallmark proposal, so you will have three "champions" per proposal). Agree on a date for each champion to submit a simple plan to implement his or her action.

    Example: A simple action to grow in the hallmark "Roots itself in Scripture" might be to purchase Bibles for the members of the church who can't afford them. The plan to support that action might be: "Research the cost and availability of ten Bibles in Dutch and four Bibles in French. Is it possible to purchase them all within my budget?"

4. Team leader collects the action plans on agreed upon date. Once the plans have been submitted, the team leader(s) evaluates each plan and suggests any needed changes. The champion for each action then implements the plan, and reports back their progress at set intervals to the team leader(s).

As we conclude this chapter we'd like to remind you once again of the definition of the *mature* dynamic: develop as a unique, local expression of the body of Christ. We do so because it is far too easy to become caught up in issues of vision, leadership, and a host of other important but secondary aspects in the life of a church to the neglect of the central truth that ought to drive us forward: the Church is God's way of continuing to embody Himself in the world. As missional church planters we are fully convinced that every local church is in some profound and mysterious way the embodiment of Christ in a specific place. That central truth is why it is essential that each community of faith wrestles to discern what "growing up" means for them.

Through the course of this chapter we've introduced you to concepts and led you through a series of learning exercises that we see as simply a good starting point to that discernment process. Regarding *maturing* we are convinced that one thing is clear: it is not a question of *if* we, the church, are to grow up but *how*. How will we, the local body of Christ, *mature* to become "The Church Beautiful" in our neighborhood? This is one of the most important discernment questions that any church leadership or planting team might ask.

And yet, *maturing* the body of Christ is so much more than what we have attempted to describe in this chapter. It involves joy and fulfillment, but also struggle and heartache and messiness, much like raising children, persevering in marriage, or making friendships work over the long haul. It involves continually learning and being adaptable to ever changing cultural and theological landscapes. Most of all *maturing* involves trusting Jesus, who is the True Builder of The Church.

Debrief: *As we've seen in this chapter,* **maturing** *is the process of developing over time as a unique, local expression of the body of Christ. More than simply an extension of* **practicing**, **maturing** *requires intentionality in four specific areas. The first area is keeping our vision updated, clear, and inspiring. Vision occurs at two levels - macro and micro. Our macro vision is for an inspiring, big-picture view of The Church Beautiful. Our micro vision is for God's dream for us as His people in our specific, local setting. The second area of intentionality is enabling and empowering every member of the body to play their part according to his or her calling and giftedness. The exercise of an individual's gifts and calling may be in service to the internal needs of the church, or it may be in living out our church's greater calling in the world.*

The third area of intentionality in our **maturing** *is in developing the depth and capacity of our church's leadership. We've explored the characteristics of Christ-like leadership and how we might identify and empower both current and potential leaders. Further, we've briefly explored how to begin to move beyond individual leaders performing individual leadership acts toward developing a leadership or governance structure. The final aspect of* **maturing** *we've covered concerns developing appropriate progress targets for our faith community. Using the Hallmarks of Maturing Church, we've looked at how to use progress targets like vehicle dashboard gauges, monitoring the health of our church as we fix our eyes on the future and move forward on mission together.*

 **MAPit!**

Turn to your Missional Action Plan in Appendix A. Go to the *Mature* section under *Strategy*. Review with your team the questions you find there in light of all of your work on the exercises in this chapter. Write down three aspects of *maturing* that you will commit to as a team. Finally, jump to the *Leadership* section under *Project*. Now that you have learned so much about leadership, how will you answer the questions you find there? Are there other more pressing issues on leadership you need to address? Feel free to write your plans there instead!

My thoughts on *Maturing*:

What are the questions that you still have about mature?

What worked well for you in this chapter?

Which parts were more difficult to grasp and why?

What needs to be addressed that is not here?

What was your takeaway thought from this chapter?

PART FOUR – GOING WIDE: EXPANDING OUR HORIZONS

As our church or project continues through the process of **practicing** *and* **maturing**, *we are beginning to realize our shared vision and grow into the community of faith that God intends us to be. We're experiencing a shared Jesus way of life together and empowering each other to exercise our gifting to build up the Body of Christ. Yet as we do this we need to be mindful that Christ's Body is not limited to our small circle. God desires that the whole world hear the good news! So how do we, a small collection of disciples in a specific locale, participate in that great work? That's where the dynamics of* **hub** *and* **extend** *come into view. These dynamics describe activities that promote the multiplication of missional initiatives and new expressions of church in and beyond our city. Let's take a look at some* **hubbing** *and* **extending** *practices to help us partner with others to seed new life near and far!*

Chapter 7 - Hub and Extend: Multiplying Life Near and Far

 This adventure has no doubt taken you down many paths you never imagined you'd tread! Your team and church have encountered so many interesting people and places in your city, and as a unique expression of the body of Christ you're learning how to wisely and patiently represent the gospel. On top of this you may be experiencing "growth pains" as you do your best to follow Jesus and mature *toward the dream God has put in your hearts. All of these experiences are worth celebrating, even those seasons when the journey seems bleak and it's hard to find your way. In this last chapter we explore what it might mean for us to continue the adventure by stepping out in faith to play our part in starting new missional initiatives and church plants. The activities behind* hub *and* extend *allow the blessing of the Kingdom to spill out in all directions, with new Christ-centered communities emerging within our city and beyond.*

HUB and EXTEND - *cultivate environments to multiply missional initiatives and churches, both locally and globally.*

What the *Hub* and *Extend* Dynamics Mean and Why They are Important

Participating with other churches, networks, and ministries brings a variety of blessings to our church. As we work with other groups, we experience collective accountability and broader access to resources. We find a place to contribute our church's unique gifts and identity for Kingdom impact and the common good. And often the discipleship of God's people is enhanced by different perspectives and connections.

Connecting and collaborating with other Christian groups undergirds the last two dynamics of Communitas' church planting approach, *hub* and *extend*. It is similar to what missionary teams do as they *embed* in their context and participate with groups beyond themselves, and as they *initiate* a coordinated gospel-sowing response. The *hub* and *extend* dynamics, however, involve more than connecting our project or church with larger networks and outside resources to sow God's *shalom*. The collaborating behind *hub* and *extend* involves a specific prioritizing of *the multiplication of new missional initiatives and churches.*

In other words, in the outworking of these two dynamics, we're not primarily aiming for goals like "multiplying disciples" or "multiplying learning communities" or even "multiplying missional movements." We in Communitas realize that these are absolutely vital aims and we must give attention to participating with others to achieve them in our city and beyond. But our endgame is more focused. Communitas' call is to move all this fruitful linking of groups in the direction of establishing churches that either directly or indirectly reproduce new churches. We tap into general multiplication environments for the specific work of cultivating church multiplication – starting faith communities in a variety of expressions that are appropriate to their context and that grow up to be whatever God intends.

As a local church builds momentum in *embedding, initiating, practicing,* and *maturing*, its vision and capacity to help resource this particular kind of multiplication will also grow. The degree to which a given church or faith community is able to participate in *hubbing* and *extending* will, of course, depend upon both its unique leadership capacity and also how strongly the lead team has each of the APEST gifts represented among them (particularly the apostolic gift). We do believe, however, that even at the earliest stages of community formation, church planting

teams ought to consider how they might help incubate new team leaders and participate in multiplying churches, both near and far. Communitas doesn't support the myth that projects should wait until they reach viability before they get involved, on some level, in new church planting.

Unlike the manner in which we covered each of the first four dynamics, we have chosen to bring our discussion of these particular two together in a single chapter. We have done this because *hub* and *extend* are two dynamics that are different primarily in their sphere of application. *Hub* involves creating or supporting local or intra-city environments to multiply missional initiatives and churches, while *extend* involves participating in inter-city and international environments that foster church planting. Given their similarity, we're covering them together in this final chapter of the guidebook.

The following descriptions might help to further clarify the difference between *hub* and *extend*:

> *Hubbing* involves those actions in our city that create or support environments for the intentional multiplication of new church planting initiatives. These environments are ideally cultivated both within the local church itself and also within the likeminded "apostolic networks" with whom the church participates across the city.[59]

> Leadership teams seek to harness both internal and external resources so that they and their key partners can provide the internships, training,

---

59 We define an "apostolic network" as an interconnected, collaborative matrix of pioneers and entrepreneurs who relate and share resources to enable the expansion, resourcing, and protection of the body of Christ and other Kingdom-minded expressions.

coaching, mentoring, and spheres for experimenting conducive to multiplying new church expressions. To hub in this dual manner, church leadership demonstrates a shrewd but humble, give-it-away perspective that puts supreme importance on Jesus' agenda for the city.

Extending involves intentionally developing wider connections and networks that reach beyond a project's or church's host city. Leadership teams collaborate and share resources across cities, nations, and continents to seed new missional initiatives and church expressions. With the outworking of this dynamic, the maturing church sees itself clearly in the light of its potential and real contribution to the global missional Body of Christ.

To help your team understand these two dynamics in practice, we have designed the following exercise, which includes the example of a Communitas church with a long history of reproducing. After the exercise, we will turn to Scripture and consider the essential element undergirding the *hub* and *extend* dynamics - collaboration. We'll then look at how our team and faith community might participate in fueling the impulse for multiplication of new missional initiatives and churches in our city and beyond.

Understanding and Applying Hub *and* Extend

Time: 2 hours
Supplies: Whiteboard, markers, sticky-notes, pens or pencils

1. Team members read the following story. Underline the parts of the story that exemplify attitudes and actions that relate to the practice of *hub* and *extend* as you understand it.

New Community's movement into church planting happened when founding pastor, Rob Fairbanks, realized they had to move from a fear-based "if we do this, it will hurt us" attitude to an "it's time to jump or we'll never do this" perspective. Within a decade after this realization, the church had been part of planting six churches. Rob describes that moment this way:

"I came to a crucial crossroads about ten years in where I realized that either I would need to mount up enough courage to do something [to move toward the dream of being a church planting church] or I would need to surrender the dream and stop talking about it. The vision I had cast was simply incompatible with the reality of our actions.

The big change came at a summer staff retreat in which we did what all church staffs do, and that is 'make plans.' It is funny how much planning happens in churches without a whole lot of results. At that time the church had three staff people: myself, the man who helped start the church, Scott Cross, and our youth pastor, Steve Hart. At the end of the retreat I pulled them aside individually and informed them that we were going to send them both out to plant churches, and they had one year to seek God's clarity on where they would plant. In retrospect, our chat was more like a hostile hostage situation. In a way, I came off like, 'You're gonna lose your job, so why not make plans to go do something awesome.' In hindsight, my proposal was just a wee bit autocratic and not very thought through. I just knew, though, that this was the time. We couldn't wait any longer. To be fair, I informed both of them that they didn't need to leave in a year, but simply had to come up with a place, and then at that time we'd forge a plan forward.

Scott almost instantly informed me with an uncomfortable smile and with firmness that he simply was not going. I'm sure Steve must have been frightened as well, but in his youthful inexperience and enthusiasm, he jumped at the opportunity. Within a few months, Steve informed me that he felt like God had revealed his will to him. I was super excited, so we dove into the conversation. Steve told me that he felt God had called him to Browne's Addition, which is a very short distance from where New Community was meeting. I have to admit that I recoiled. I am seriously competitive, and the success of New Community came with much toil and hard work. I often joke that our church was 'a 10-year overnight success.' Planting a church is not easy. A veteran missionary I know calls church planting the 'X Games of Christian ministry.' Honestly, I felt threatened. I thought to myself, 'Go find your own damn people. You're gonna kill our church.' Earlier you might have been thinking, 'Rob is a truly spiritual person.' Well, I am glad that myth is put to bed. Anyway, the fact is, I loved Steve. I have always felt that he is one of the truly anointed young leaders—at least of the ones I have met. I felt like everyone from our church would go with him. Heck, I liked Steve so much I wanted to go with him.

What helped me was the sagely advice of a fellow pastor, Joe Wittwer. He had already planted several churches from his church and counseled me to take a Kingdom approach. He felt so strongly about this that he believed he could plant a new church in his building because the giftings of the new community would be so different from his that both communities would and could thrive, reaching a whole new group of people. Jesus encouraged us to seek his Kingdom first. Joe embodied that for me. That said, we began to make a plan to start a new community a mere stone's throw away."[60]

"I used to believe you needed to get to a certain size to reproduce," Rob shares. "New Community engaged in its first church plant only after it had grown to about 500 people. Now, my experience teaches me that it's more about finding leaders interested in planting and investing in them than it is about size and momentum. Churches can be involved in planting a lot sooner than I used to believe."

New Community has not only sent out its own leaders to start churches, but has been involved in Kingdom alliances with other churches and organizations, including Whitworth College and Communitas, for the purpose of sowing God's shalom. These apostolic networks have served as fishing pools for those feeling stirred to church plant in the city and beyond.

One particular apostolic network that New Community played a significant role in developing over the past ten years is "Ecclesia Spokane." What originally started as a regular lunch gathering of local planters and pastors desiring connections with other local leaders, grew, with Rob's fueling, into a community of pioneering

---

60 Russ Davis, "Creating Multiplication Movements," *Grow Where You're Planted*, Eds. Daniel Steigerwald and Kelly Crull (Portland: Christian Associates Press, 2013), 237-239.

leaders. These leaders not only consistently share their lives, but scheme together to see how God's goodness might be spread across Spokane. Often they interact over best practices for starting missional initiatives and churches, and now those facilitating Ecclesia's development hope the group can continue to be not only a community of lead planters and pastors but an ongoing catalyst for church planting.

And the story continues. At the time of this writing Communitas, New Community Spokane, and a rural Mexican church planting group are exploring an opportunity to place a church planter from Mexico into New Community for training in urban ministry. The hope is that upon completion of the training, the planter would return to Mexico and launch the group's first church plant in an urban center.[61]

2. In groups of four or less, share your underlines. Note the behaviors that are distinctly *hubbing* activities with an 'H', and those that are clearly *extending* activities with an 'E.'

3. Compare and contrast your church's behavior to what you've noted in the story above. Discuss the following questions, first with a focus on *hubbing* activities and then with a focus on *extending* activities:
   - *What questions do you have about* hubbing *and* extending?
   - *How might the specific attitudes and behaviors found in the story also apply to your church's hubbing/extending?*
   - *What is unique to your church or project's practice of* hub/extend *currently?*
   - *What would be your ideal* hub/extend *practice? Brainstorm some specific actions your team might take to deliberately hub/extend. It's okay to be imaginative or tentative about your ideas, as you will be updating them later.*

   From your list of ideas select two actions for *hub* and one for *extend*. Write each action on a sticky-note.

4. Gathered as a team, groups take turns posting their sticky-notes on the whiteboard and presenting their actions. Facilitator arranges the sticky-notes into two groups: one for *hubbing* actions and the second for *extending*. After each group has shared, select two or three *hubbing* actions you would like to take on as a team, as well as one *extending* action. Make a simple plan to implement these actions and schedule a time to evaluate your actions and outcomes.

---

61 This account is based on an interview with Rob Fairbanks.

Hubbing and *extending* describe discerned participation in multiplying new missional initiatives and churches. In the case of New Community Church, we see that local churches sometimes create the *hubbing* dynamic within the church itself. However, Communitas finds that the birthing of new church expressions more commonly takes the collaborative energy of several groups. Even New Community, though gifted with a strong apostolic point leader, recognized the wisdom and advantage of tapping into a wider network to foster new church planting. What's most important is to take the steps to *hub* and *extend* that make the most sense for you. The rest of the chapter is designed to assist you toward that end.

The Call to Collaborate for Kingdom Impact

Hub and *extend*, while primarily focused on creating new church expressions, also protect the people of God from a danger inherent to any group of impassioned people: limiting its activities and field of relationships to a familiar circle or camp. All of us prefer operating within the familiar silo of our given church, denomination, or whatever we define as our primary tribe. And therein lies the problem. Over time, we can get saturated in the water of our sameness. We may even begin to think we're rather elite or cutting-edge compared to other groups or networks. We imagine that we've got all that we need internally - leadership savvy, finances, books, etc. - to keep us learning what we need to learn. Sometimes we even go so far as to practically worship popular leaders.

The slide into isolation often happens unconsciously, but it can lead our community to limit nearly all contact with other groups who follow the same Jesus simply because their ways seem foreign or strange to us. Unfortunately, this separatist mentality ends up

limiting our group's needed contribution to enriching God's collective work in our city and beyond. And it can stifle our *maturing* as well.

In the city of Corinth, the Apostle Paul in his day had to address such segmenting of the local body of Christ into separate, oftentimes competing, factions. This ailment is not exclusive to our era! In his first letter to the Corinthians, Paul strongly rebukes the church in Corinth for separating themselves into uniform groups under apostolic leaders like Apollos, Cephas, and Paul himself.

At the beginning of I Corinthians, Paul mentions at least four factions of Christians operating in Corinth. Here's an important point that is often missed regarding Paul's exhortation: Paul is *not* chastening the Corinthians for dividing themselves into specific camps. He doesn't say, "quit organizing yourself into distinct groups." While Paul doesn't explicitly argue in favor of this in the passage, it can be healthy for groups, organizations, denominations, etc. to differentiate themselves by creating their own tribal style, culture, theological distinctives, and approach to discipleship. And groups often emerge with a key leader or two who become prominent. This is quite normal. What angered Paul the most about the situation in Corinth, however, was that each camp was forgetting one key reality: they were all meant to be working under the common banner of Jesus, attempting to demonstrate and proclaim the same Kingdom under Christ. Paul strongly exhorts them: "Is Christ divided? Was Paul crucified for you? Were you baptized in the name of Paul?" (1:7).

In chapters three and four of I Corinthians Paul urges these Christian camps to quit comparing themselves one to another (3:3-4; 4:6-7), and especially, to stop boasting in their leaders and about their particular group's superiority versus the other Christian groups in the city (3:5-7, 18-23; 4:6-7). They collectively - all of them together - represent God's field. Paul and

Apollos and Cephas each have their own part in cultivating that field, as do each of the Corinthians. In his argument Paul also resorts to yet another metaphor to emphasize how critical it is for all camps to work together to build one sacred, living structure - God's people as a collective "temple:"

16 *"Don't you know that you yourselves are God's temple and that God's Spirit dwells in your midst?* 17 *If anyone destroys God's temple, God will destroy that person; for God's temple is sacred, and you **together** are that temple."* - I Cor. 3:16-17 (emphasis added)

Unfortunately, unity of purpose remains quite uncommon among diverse groups of Christians. Humble, patient, and persevering efforts bring such groups together to achieve good Kingdom ends. Though we know it is hard work, we also know that for Christ's sake, it is worth it. The next exercise will help you develop a "Collaboration Covenant" a simple tool to maintain focus on God's greater work in your city and in the world.

Creating a Collaboration Covenant

Time: 2 hours
Supplies: Bibles, paper, pens or pencils

1. Gather into small groups of four or less. Each person reads I Corinthians 1-4 and writes a one paragraph reflection on collaboration based on Paul's exhortation in the passage. Allow 20 to 30 minutes for this step.

    Example:

    As a leadership team we will hold each other accountable to keep Jesus and the Kingdom in view in all our decision-making. We will strive to honor and respect our sisters and brothers operating in our city in Jesus' name, and will resist harboring a competitive, non-cooperative spirit. At the same time we will embrace our calling and lead our community into its unique expression, while also giving preferred attention to supporting those church and network partners that have values and vision complementary to ours. We appreciate the body of Christ in its many-sided beauty in our city, and we accept that this mosaic of unity under Jesus helps us move closer to the unity Jesus describes in John 17:20-21. We also recognize that we don't have to agree on every point with others in order to be able to work fruitfully and shrewdly alongside them.

2. When prompted, each person will pass their paper to the left and receive a paper from their right. Participants read their neighbor's paper, making comments and adding thoughts. Repeat the process every five minutes until you have read a paper from each person at your table and you receive back your own paper. Read what has been added to your paragraph.

3.   Using a large sheet of paper, work together to combine the individual reflections into a single "Collaboration Covenant" for the small group. Then write a list of three to five actions you might take to live it out.

Example:

How we will live:
- We will intentionally set aside a time of retreat at least once a year to pray and discern specifically how Jesus might have us involved in multiplying new missional initiatives and churches in our city and beyond.
- We will compare and contrast the gifts and callings on our leadership team, and decide who is best suited to keep our apostolic eyes outward. And we will empower this leader to keep our participation active in church planting and other initiatives by assigning him/her specific times to share vision and opportunities with both our leadership team and also with our church.
- We will tap into Communitas and Forge as apostolic networks, and we will seek to identify local leaders, churches, and ministries that have a specific passion to see new expressions of church started in our city.

4.   Coming together as the team, a representative from each group will read their group's Collaboration Covenant and actions.

5.   After each group's work has been shared, the facilitator recruits three team members to synthesize a Collaboration Covenant, including theory and action. Set a date to review the team's results.

Let's now look at how we might direct a Kingdom perspective and collaborative stance toward birthing new missional initiatives and churches.

Fueling the Impulse for Multiplication

Leadership teams need to regularly discern how their faith communities might factor into God's grand work in and beyond their respective cities. If we take following Jesus seriously, there's no escaping the call to collaborate for Kingdom gain!

Such Kingdom-oriented efforts may surprise us in terms of what the Spirit can do to bring about new expressions of church. All our *hubbing* and *extending* activities have that hopeful goal in view of multiplying missional initiatives and context-appropriate churches.

Communitas' apostolic calling as an organization means we approach this purpose with great passion. We do realize, however, that our project teams may not harbor such an unwavering zeal to see new churches multiplied. Each team will need to articulate their own reasons why they ought to participate in new church planting in their city and beyond. Through the help of this guidebook we hope your team has not only latched onto a dream of the "Church Beautiful," but has begun to imagine how many beautiful churches could bless God and change lives everywhere. In our experience, most churches who do participate in church planting find the experience generative for their own community. With such positives in mind, let's look briefly at characteristics of reproducing churches and then explore practical ways to participate with others in establishing new missional initiatives and churches.

Identifying Characteristics of Reproducing Churches

Robert Vajko, a long-term church planter in France, studied reproducing churches from several denominations operating in France. His research revealed the fourteen characteristics included in the list below. We don't have the space in this book to develop each characteristic, nor would we necessarily advocate for some of them. However we include the list as a catalyst for discussion on your leadership team.

Characteristics of French churches that reproduced:
1. A vision for reproduction
2. Willing to take risks
3. A spirit of self-giving
4. Are themselves growing as a church
5. Know how to plant daughter churches
6. Sensitive to the Spirit of God
7. Finances not central
8. Care for the training of their own church planters
9. Leadership base multiplied
10. A Pauline vision
11. Receptive areas sought
12. Homogeneous populations targeted
13. Creativity is encouraged
14. Clear principles[62]

It's interesting to note that in addition to these characteristics, Vajko also discovered that "churches that are part of a fellowship of churches tend to reproduce themselves more than independent churches. My study of reproducing churches showed that the most reproductive churches, not surprisingly, were part of a movement that encouraged reproduction."[63]

Sam Metcalf, author of *Beyond the Local Church*, puts it this way: "Planting churches never guarantees that a movement will result, but generating healthy movements will always result in new church expressions."[64] We in Communitas believe that this movement includes ministries, seminaries, other nonprofit entities, and Christian-led businesses that form broad alliances with churches to multiply churches. This may even be the preferred way to start churches, since these broader coalitions tend to give church plant team leaders exposure to a greater pool of ideas, giftedness, and resources. In addition, including team leaders in a fellowship of church planters in the city (such as Ecclesia Spokane mentioned earlier in the chapter) can enrich the development of churches perhaps more profoundly than any other approach.

Tapping into Apostolic Networks

In Communitas we believe that a host of different kinds of partnerships are needed to see incarnational churches multiplied that make new and better

---

62 Craig Ott and Gene Wilson, *Global Church Planting* (Grand Rapids: Baker Academic, 2011), 293.

63 As quoted in Ott and Wilson, *Global Church Planting*, 299.

64 Sam Metcalf, *Beyond the Local Church: How Apostolic Movements Can Change the World* (Downers Grove: InterVarsity Press, 2015), 80.

disciples. But we also recognize the wisdom of intentionally tapping into the reproductive energy of apostolic networks over the life of a church. These particular kinds of networks tend to be filled with entrepreneurial, risk-taking people (in other words, apostolic, prophetic, and evangelistic types), and may be one of the best ways to help faith communities get involved in multiplying new missional initiatives and churches. *Being strategically selective in this way is particularly important for teams who struggle to find adequate representation of the apostolic gift within their leadership core in any given season.*

One example of an apostolic network that is becoming a catalyzing agent for activating the *hubbing* and *extending* dynamics in a number of different countries is the Forge Mission Training Network (http://forgeinternational.com/). Communitas is blessed to partner with Forge on a global level. As the name suggests, this network is about forging alliances among churches, seminaries, denominations, pioneering groups, etc. for the purpose of creating environments to train and multiply missionaries and missional communities. Forge effectively trains local missionaries toward the multiplication of missional communities, which may or may not be attached to existing churches. Communitas can then offer additional coaching, training, and support

to these missional communities as they aim to grow into sustainable, reproducing churches. Sometimes Communitas staff or churches also start Forge Training Hubs in new cities to catalyze local missional movement. As an example of this in practice, the primary author of this guidebook, Dan Steigerwald, started a hub in Portland, Oregon several years ago, and is seeing first-hand how such a local network can be a seedbed for incubating church planters.

Cultivating Our Gifts for **Hubbing and** Extending

Another way your team can encourage a reproductive posture is by continually providing voice and influence to people in your midst with apostolic, prophetic, and evangelistic (APE) gifts (see Alan Hirsch's definitions of these gifts in chapter six of this workbook). Let's consider the way the APEST gifts commonly find expression in the life of churches that succeed in reproducing new churches. Although they don't use the full scope of the APEST language, Craig Ott and Gene Wilson, in their book, *Global Church Planting* (2011), touch upon the way these gifts are typically expressed in the life of churches that actually reproduce (see figure 4):

Figure 4
Critical Spiritual Gifts for the Developmental Phases[65]

Gifts of Apostle & Evangelist	Reproducing
Gifts of Admin & Leadership	Structuring
Gifts of Pastor & Teacher	Establishing
Gifts of Apostle & Evangelist	Launching

---

65 Ott and Wilson, *Global Church Planting*, 164 (Figure used by permission).

Notice in the diagram that the apostolic and evangelistic gifts are commonly operative at startup ("launching"), and then they subside in emphasis until some later developmental phase which the authors label "reproducing." Though the prophetic gift is not represented in this paradigm, the depiction above demonstrates a fairly common way new church development is viewed. The outward-focused gifts (APE) and the inward-focused gifts (ST) are expressed over the life of a church, but not during the same seasons. As the diagram shows, after the initial launching phase the outward energy typically drops off and is followed by a long inward period comprised of the establishing and structuring phases. Over time - long after the church has reached viability - this structuring phase gives way to a fresh outward phase where the reproducing energy is somehow resurrected.

As tidy as the above diagram looks on paper, in reality few churches manage to recover the initial APE energy when it is allowed to subside in the middle phases. In that long season devoted to internal development and structuring (which is good and important work!), church leaders err in that they consistently believe their community is not quite strong or savvy enough to endure a birth just yet. That belief, if unchecked, can not only neuter a church's reproductive capacity for the long haul, but it can also fuel fears that even partnering with others to plant new churches would be too depleting to undertake.

In their study of church planting across the globe, Ott and Wilson offer this warning about the common tapering-off of the outward energy as new churches become established:

> "Often by the time the church has matured to a point of considering reproduction, the members are weary and want to rest and enjoy the fruits of their labors... Many will have the impression that there is work enough just sustaining the gains that have been made during the young life of the church. Such concerns and fatigue are fully understandable but can lead to stagnation and spiritual lethargy if allowed to become a dominant spirit."[66]

When members have become so wearied from the ups and downs of church planting, re-injecting the outward energy at some later stage in the church's maturing process requires a great deal of prayer, vision, and finesse by leadership. Perhaps this is why so few churches reproduce.

We believe that this four-stage portrayal above (figure 4) may in fact be too limiting as a pattern to follow for natural church development and reproduction. For one, we're suggesting that church development need not be viewed as such a linear process, with reproduction as the capstone after years and years of *maturing* the mother. In Communitas' experience we find a good number of young churches that activate reproductive energy even as they build their own faith communities. For example, by seeding missional initiatives that practice *communion*, *community*, and *mission* (the base elements of "church" as described in the Introduction), a newly forming church can generate new expressions that can themselves grow into new churches. The story we read in chapter one about the replication of churches in Spain attests to this possibility.

Secondly, we believe that it is possible to keep the APEST gifts in balanced activation over the life of the church. Through the exercise in the previous chapter on **Creating an Atmosphere of APEST Collaboration in Leadership**, your team defined a way to integrate APEST into your team's regular decision-making

---

66 Ibid., 292-293.

process. This, along with other intentional actions, can help a church to reproduce, or at minimum, stay engaged with others beyond the church to multiply new missional initiatives and churches.

Finally, it's important to note that this balancing of the internal nurturing gifts (Shepherd-Teacher) with the outward entrepreneurial gifts (Apostle-Prophet-Evangelist) is rarely if ever secured apart from substantial conflict between members of the leadership team. Few of us enjoy conflict; in fact most of us seek to avoid it. Yet from Communitas' vantage point, resolving this conflict by enabling one faction to dominate the other is not the solution. Living into the tension rather than seeking to eradicate it is the better approach.

Innovating Where the Spirit is Leading

When it comes to multiplying new churches, we need to learn from wisdom and experience, but also be open for innovating where the Spirit is leading. At times God leads teams to reproduce churches in very uncommon ways. In Poland, for example, Paul Haenze and his network are witnessing the beginnings of what could become a church planting movement that's growing out of the soil of homeless shelters! Paul relates this story:

Over the past decade God has enabled Daniel Wolkiewicz to travel a road he never imagined he'd be on. His denomination sent him to plant a church in a town of 40,000 in southern Poland, but despite his best efforts a church did not get planted. But somewhere along the way, God revealed another way to move toward Daniel's dream of church planting. With the surprising provision of a large vacant building, Daniel and his family were able to start a ministry to the homeless that has since grown to be the one of the largest of its type in Poland. His ministry centers now house hundreds of people every day, serve over half a million hot meals every year, and provide job training for dozens of people at a time.

During the establishing of that first ministry center, Daniel defined a process of spiritual formation for his guests. By intentionally discipling people, over time Daniel has managed to raise up the leaders and resources needed to multiply many ministry centers. Along the way Daniel realized these centers could be ideal opportunities for starting new churches. God enabled him to test this vision, and today several new churches are growing in the soil of these centers. Ironically, the church in that first homeless facility has planted a church in the very community where Daniel was originally sent to plant a church fifteen years ago.

Daniel has recently adopted a new approach from CityTeam International. He is presently teaching homeless men and women a simple approach to start churches in new areas. These volunteers are preparing to go into the surrounding villages and towns. His desire is to see churches multiply throughout his region. It's amazing to see the way God has used Daniel to plant churches in a most unconventional way.

Many teams find ways to organically birth new churches that demand much less than what we typically imagine is needed for church multiplication. Various "simple church" networks and house church networks, for example, provoke the multiplication of additional communities. They tend to be nimbler forms of church, lower in complexity, and do not require the organizational systems and leadership that other forms of church might need.

In some cases, as we saw with New Community in Spokane, individual churches may be able to create the *hubbing* dynamic within the circle of their own faith community. This is often done by recruiting and grooming a pioneering leader or two to start and multiply several missional communities or small groups. The host church essentially creates an environment for entrepreneur-types to be mentored, resourced, and sent out to experiment. Over time, those point leaders form teams and operate clusters of groups that can be spun off to form new churches. In Troy Cady's earlier telling of Communitas' story in Madrid, Spain, we see the power of this kind of serial planting, where Mountainview Church helped foster the birth of Oasis, which in turn helped daughter Decoupage, and now a new missional initiative, *Poieme Collectiva*, beyond Madrid in the city of Valencia.

Many young church plants fail to see that they themselves can be the best kind of incubator for new church planters. Larger churches are typically the ones that provide internships for prospective planters, and too often these focus on interns learning how to run a full-orbed church rather than obtaining the skills and perspectives needed for pioneer planting. What better place for "green" leaders to learn about planting than in the wild, liminal space of a new church plant!

Too many established churches hub locally by defaulting to the "easier way" to church plant. They intentionally send a group of their members to "colonize" an area, as if church reproduction is mostly about cloning the mother. On a pragmatic level, this can get the job done, and no doubt it works superbly in some cases. Too often, however, this approach to planting stifles the new church's capacity to make disciples, as colonizing commonly skips or only superficially engages the work of *embedding*, *initiating*, and *practicing*. But, if done with these other dynamics in operation, sending a sizeable group from one or more visible local churches to inhabit an area can work without compromising discipleship and sensitivity to context.

All this to say, there are many ways to *hub* and *extend* for the sake of multiplying missional initiatives and churches. We encourage teams to seek the Spirit's guidance as they together discern their own unique way(s) to be involved in establishing new expressions of church. The metric of success is faithfulness to what you as a leadership team sense that God is calling you to do. Though there are many ways to start new churches, one thing we're quite sure about: multiplication of new church expressions rarely happens by accident. It requires deliberate practices that are worth cultivating at the earliest stages of a project or church's development.

As mentioned earlier, one important practice is partnering with local entities for multiplication. We have designed the following multi-part exercise to help your team begin the journey of finding local partners.

Finding Local Partners to Help Multiply Missional Initiatives and Churches

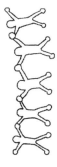

Time: Five sessions, 60-90 minutes each plus additional time to implement action steps
Supplies: As required in each part of the exercise

This exercise guides you through various steps including outside research, meetings with potential partners, and work within the team to begin helpful partnerships.

Part 1: Individual Preparation
Time: 60 minutes

Each team member prepares of a list of four to five prospective local partners by researching either online or in-person suitable local networks or personal connections, organizations, and churches. Pay special attention to apostolic networks.

Part 2: Team Preparation
Time: 60 minutes
Supplies: Copies of your Collaboration Covenant from the learning exercise earlier in this chapter, whiteboard and markers

1. Read aloud your Collaboration Covenant.

2. Each team member "introduces" their list of prospective partners to the larger group and writes the names on the whiteboard. Through discernment and discussion, the team decides on a few prospective partnerships for starting new missional initiatives and churches.

3. Pairs from the team volunteer to visit prospective partners on the list. Determine a date when your team will meet and assess findings.

Part 3: Pair Interviews
Time: 60 minutes per interview

Pairs from the team meet with their assigned prospective partner.

1. Prepare for the interview. Take time to pray, remind yourself what it is you're hoping to gain from this conversation, and give some forethought to the questions you would like to ask the prospective partner. Possible questions include:
    *   *How do you see God at work in your area of influence?*

- *What kind of outcomes are you hoping for through your work and organization?*
- *Where do you feel your greatest strengths lie?*
- *What are you lacking to achieve your outcomes, and how could collaboration help advance your work?*
- *You may also wish to review Appendix D: Asking Open Questions prior to your visit.*

2. Meet with your prospective partner. In your conversation:
   - Focus on being an active listener, asking questions that show your interest while also affirming the good that you're hearing. Remind yourself to be slow to critique, and not to jump to conclusions about their ministry.
   - Share your interest in collaborating and some initial ideas of what you might like to see happen in working together. Consider sharing your Collaboration Covenant. After you share, invite the person's feedback about what they see as possibilities for working together.

3. Debrief your interview. Where a connection looks promising for collaborating, evaluate the prospect in light of the following criteria:
   - *To what degree are we in harmony on group identity (mission/calling, vision, values, theology, etc.)?*
   - *What goals or purposes do we share in common that would focus our work together?*
   - *To what extent do we have good relational chemistry as potential partners, and who else is key to this partnership that we might need to meet?*
   - *How do our group's competencies and gifts complement those of this prospective partner, and what could each of us be responsible for in terms of partnering toward multiplying missional initiatives and churches?*

4. Email members of your team a report of your findings and recommendations.

Part 4: Team Discernment
Time: 90 minutes
Supplies: Whiteboard and markers

1. As the team gathers, each pair shares the results of their visit with their assigned prospective partner along with their recommendations. The facilitator records findings on the whiteboard. After each pair has shared, spend a few minutes in prayer for the prospective partner and asking God for wisdom to discern opportunities for collaboration.

2. After all have shared, ask to what extent any of the prospective partnerships seem "right and good to us and the Holy Spirit" – what is our praying and discerning telling us, or how is God nudging us?

3. As a team, select one or two prospective partners for starting new missional initiatives and churches. Designate at least two members from your team, perhaps including the team's point leader, to meet with these partners and discuss collaboration plans. Details should include:
   - *Toward what outcomes or goals will you work together?*
   - *How will you develop functional relationships with the partner? How will you approach issues of leadership, conflict, responsibility, and trust?*
   - *Who will be responsible for the collaboration?*

4. Set a date to meet for part five of this exercise.

Part 5: Next Actions
Time: 60 minutes

1. Team gathers to listen to those who did visits report on their findings. Describe how your team is able to collaborate with each partner.

2. Prayerfully decide with whom your team will partner.

3. Team designates a point leader for the partnership who recruits a team as necessary and creates an action plan that details the steps you wish to take to collaborate with the partner.

4. Implement the plan with your partner and report back to the team as needed.

Staying On the Path Through Coaching

We recognize that what we're encouraging in this chapter is very difficult. When every kind of complexity is hitting you as a team who are just trying to get your own project started, it's really hard to give serious attention to multiplying new churches. To help you be deliberate about robustly participating in *hubbing* and *extending*, we recommend that you regularly connect with a strategic coach, preferably one who is an experienced church planter. If you have a single point leader, encourage them to secure such a coach. In the absence of a team leader, decide who on your team you would like to meet regularly with that coach.

We have included below a group of representative questions a strategic coach might ask to help your leadership team keep multiplication visible on your dashboard. Your team may find it helpful to keep these questions visible even at the earliest stages of your project. In closing this chapter, we have developed an exercise around these questions to help your team better understand *hub* and *extend* and stimulate you to add more specific *hubbing* and *extending* actions to your unique Collaboration Covenant for the season ahead.

Stimulating More Actions to Deepen Our Hubbing and Extending

Time: 2 hours
Supplies: Large sheets of paper, markers, tape, writing paper, pens or pencils, your team's
Collaboration Covenant

Prior to this exercise write the HUB and EXTEND questions below on large sheets of paper - one sheet for the HUB questions and the other for EXTEND. Display them on the wall.

1. Read to the group the displayed questions below. These are questions that an experienced coach might process with a team or church desiring to *hub* and *extend*.

    HUB
    - How are you creating environments that develop both leaders that build the internal strength of the church and also leaders that move the body into involvement in multiplying missional initiatives and churches?
    - Where are you cultivating a presence (e.g. a density of groups or missional initiatives) among a people group or area in your city that could lead to new church planting?
    - Who can you approach to regularly coach your team that has experience in church planting and who regularly coaches diverse church planting teams?
    - What training processes, internships, and missional experimenting are you engaging in to prevent the natural tendency to turn inward (e.g. a Forge Residency)?
    - What local compassion and justice initiatives are you active in that might "shake out" leaders who could potentially lead a new church plant?

    EXTEND
    - What would it take to establish a global partnership or to "adopt a city" to create a cross-cultural learning community for fostering church planting? What resources, people, and funds are you committing to church planting?
    - Who is God giving you, or who is attracted to you that might be challenged to serve in multiplying initiatives and churches cross-culturally beyond your city or country, and how are you cultivating those people?
    - What opportunities are you creating for leaders, planters, interns, etc. to be exposed to and acquire your DNA so that they might infuse it elsewhere beyond your city?
    - What is your investment in other churches in your networks beyond your city? Which of these churches desires to become more missional and postured for church planting?

2. The team collects into two working groups: one will address the HUB questions, the other will consider the EXTEND questions. Each group decides on two questions they would like to address from their list.

3. For each chosen question, discuss and note your responses to these prompts:
    *   *What are we currently doing to address this question?*
    *   *What should we start doing to address this question?*
    *   *What should we stop doing that will allow us to address this question?*

    Write a brief group response to each question.

4. Come together as a team to share your *hub* and *extend* responses. Develop the actions you will take in the next year to see those questions adequately addressed. Add these actions to your Collaboration Covenant.

    As an optional step, consider appointing two "champions" - one for *hubbing* activities and one for *extending* activities - to lead the charge and hold the team accountable for *hubbing* and *extending* in the next year.

We believe that as your community begins to partner with others in and beyond your city, you will find *hubbing* and *extending* to be rewarding and helpful in ways that may surprise you. Although in this chapter we have emphasized how these actions will foster the multiplication of new churches, we also experience numerous other blessings in the process: diversity, resources, camaraderie, accountability, encouragement, and support. In light of these great benefits, we strongly encourage your team, regardless of size or maturity, to lean into *hubbing* and *extending* in ways that are appropriate for you.

As we bring this chapter to a close, let us again stress that for any team, project, or church, faithfulness to God is the most important measure of success. We know that *hubbing* and *extending* must never be seen as a rigid, one-size-fits-all prescription but as the result of fruitful discernment. The learning exercises throughout this chapter have led you to develop multiple actions for *hubbing* and *extending*. Such practices are intended to be a blessing, not a burden. We encourage you to implement them.

Debrief: *In this final chapter of the workbook we've considered how our project or church might begin the process of starting new missional initiatives and churches by* **hubbing** *and* **extending.** *As with* **maturing,** **hubbing** *and* **extending** *require a great deal of intentionality. Keeping those with APE (apostolic, prophetic, and evangelistic) giftings activated throughout the lifecycle of the church will ensure that the impulse to push outward will always be present in our faith community, challenging us to be mindful of ministry opportunities "out there" even as we disciple those already in our church. We've seen through the example of New Community Church in Spokane that there is no proper "time" to multiply, rather that multiplication stems from vision, intention, and the development of leaders in step with the leading of the Holy Spirit.*

We've given you some practical tips and exercises to not only begin **hubbing** *and* **extending** *but also to maintain a multiplying posture for the long haul. Creating a Collaboration Covenant is a great start. A further step is to live into your Collaboration Covenant by connecting with other churches, organizations, and apostolic networks to discover potential ministry partners and discerning how the Spirit leads you to collaboration. Finally, as with all of the dynamics of missional church planting,* **hubbing** *and* **extending** *should align with God's unique design of your local Body of Christ.*

 MapIt!

Turn to your Missional Action Plan in Appendix A. Go to the *Collaboration Covenant* section and write out your team's final version from the ***Creating a Collaboration Covenant*** learning exercise. Then go to the *Hub* section under *Strategy* and review with your team the questions you find there. What are the *hubbing* activities your team has committed to in your Collaboration Covenant? What *hubbing* actions did you develop in the ***Stimulating More Actions to Deepen Our Hubbing and Extending*** learning exercise? Write three responses in the space provided. Repeat the process for the *Extend* section of your MAP.

My Thoughts on *Hubbing* and *Extending*:

What are the questions that you still have about hub and extend?

What worked well for you in this chapter?

Which parts were more difficult to grasp and why?

What needs to be addressed that is not here?

What was your takeaway thought from this chapter?

Dynamic Adventure

EPILOGUE

Congratulations! You've made your way to the final page of this guidebook! Wherever you find yourself at this moment, we offer you these words of encouragement: *Embrace the Dynamic Adventure that God has called you to!* Lean into the wild and unpredictable adventure that is missional church planting.

As you follow God into context, the road will twist and turn unexpectedly. Around every corner there will be something new. Sometimes there will be great, unforeseen joy. Other times there will be deep challenges. There may be hills to climb that seem to grow taller with each step you take. Your traveling companions may come and go suddenly. Yet through it all take comfort in knowing that God has set your feet on this path, and He knows what lies ahead. Trust Him as you journey forward, always mindful that faithfulness to God is the primary measure of success.

At the same time, use the tools we've given you – the MAP, the three elements of church, the twelve hallmarks, and especially the six dynamics themselves - to get a reading on your location and help you to determine your next step on the adventure. Sometimes a GPS can be your best friend amidst the chaos of a crowded city. Pressing that little "find my location" button can be really helpful! Our hope is that this workbook will serve that purpose for you.

We encourage you to keep this book close at hand and invite you to use it in any way that best serves your mission. As your project or church moves through different seasons, revisit the appropriate chapters. Use the learning exercises to once again spark your imagination. Adapt them and experiment with them to suit your team and context.

Finally, whether you are just beginning to *embed* and *initiate* in a new context, are helping your church to *practice* and *mature*, or are working through the process of *hubbing* and *extending*, we encourage you to press on! Press on because the world needs to know Jesus.

In Communitas we believe that many people will come to know Jesus by first meeting Him in churches that think, act, and care like Him. The kingdom needs all varieties, all forms, and all expressions of church for all kinds of people. So whatever your context, whatever your specific mission, press on. Press on so that your cherished friends, family, and neighbors can meet Jesus in The Church Beautiful.

"Now to him who is able to do immeasurably more than all we ask or imagine, according to his power that is at work within us, to him be glory in the church and in Christ Jesus throughout all generations, for ever and ever! Amen."
– Ephesians 3:20-21

A *Dynamic Adventure* is best experienced with others! Our hope is that you will walk through this workbook together with a local group of dreamers, practitioners, or church planters excited to make a difference in your city with the good news of Jesus. We invite you to participate in the worldwide community forming at www.thedynamicadventure.com where you'll find a growing collection of additional material, training, videos, and coaching. At thedynamicadventure.com you'll find a great place to connect with other adventurers to share stories and best practices from your very own *Dynamic Adventure!*

APPENDICES

Appendix A

 The Missional Action Plan

PROJECT INFO
Project Name:
Project Team Leader:
Project Team Members:
Project website:

Introduction:

The Missional Action Plan (or MAP) is a tool designed to help your project flourish. The purpose of the MAP is to guide you through a series of important concepts and practices to help bring clarity and focus to your current activities and future plans. We find that periodically pausing to ask, "what are we doing, and why?" is quite helpful to most church planting teams. With that in mind, remember the MAP is intended to serve you – you don't serve it. It's not designed to be a rigid and unbending taskmaster. It's a place for *your* team to write down *your* ideas for *your* project in *your* context. Take time to think and dream together as a team, and then write down your ideas and intentions below.

The MAP is also a great tool to spark interaction with your coach. By writing down your ideas and intentions, your coach can have a better sense of what your team hopes to accomplish. From there she can help you evaluate your goals and help ensure that your activities and actions are aligned with them.

Instructions:

Your MAP is a living document. It is meant to change over time as your project grows and changes. This is a printed document designed to help your team get its initial ideas and intentions down "on paper." As your ideas take shape and your action steps become clearer, we encourage you to work with your coach to develop an electronic version that you can edit and share more easily. And it's important that you review your MAP periodically to keep it fresh. A shareable electronic copy is likely a better way to accomplish that.

Keep your answers short and to the point. Brief answers will keep your plans "do-able." Long answers are often harder to implement, so your MAP should not exceed about three pages. Take the amount of time you need to process well with your team. Some answers may come easy to you and others may not. That's to be expected, so take all the time you need. Whatever your process, we hope you find this exercise helpful.

VISION STATEMENT
What is the vision for your project or church? Write it down here. A short, realistic-but-faith-based statement is best with no more than 3 to 5 sentences.

STRATEGY

Over the next year or two what do you want to see accomplished – and how? To help you process your strategy we've included the six dynamics of our missional church planting approach. Use the prompts to think of simple, attainable activities for each dynamic that pertains to your current situation. If you're not "there yet" for a few of the dynamics, use that section to dream on paper. Try to give short, specific answers.

Embed – How is your team *embedding* and building key relationships in your context? What's currently working? What's not? What would you like to do?

1.
2.
3.

Initiate – How is your team embodying and proclaiming the gospel in your context? What's currently working? What's not? What would you like to do? What has been the result of your team discernment process?

1.
2.
3.

Practice – What is the identity (vision and values) and way of life you are practicing together that you intend to invite others into? Have you processed that together? What's currently working? What's not? What do you need to change or start doing to see discipleship happen?

1.
2.
3.

Mature – How are you organizing as a people so that the body is empowered to make more and better disciples? How will you work toward sustainability? What's currently working? What's not? What do you need to change or start doing to see discipleship, health, and sustainability happen?

1.
2.
3.

Hub – How are you creating an environment for multiplication of new initiatives or churches across your local area and city? What people or networks do you know that you could connect with for that purpose? What's currently working? What's not? What do you need to start doing to see local church planting happen?

1.
2.
3.

Extend – How are you fueling missional movement and the development of new churches or initiatives beyond your city? What people or networks do you know that you could connect with for that purpose? What's currently working? What's not? What do you need to start doing to see trans-local church planting happen?

1.
2.
3.

The "Basics" of Church
How do you intend to express the three basic functions in your faith community?

Communion
How will your faith community relate corporately to God? What are you doing now? What would you like to do? What will that look like?

1.
2.
3.

Community
How do the people in your faith community relate to each other? How will you deepen relationships to embody the gospel of grace together? What are you doing now? What would you like to do? What will that look like?

1.
2.
3.

Mission

How will your faith community relate to its host community? What redemptive purposes will it pursue in your city? What are you doing now? What would you like to do? What will that look like?

1.
2.
3.

Project

A healthy Communitas project should develop to a place where it leads itself and sustains itself financially. Even if you are very early in the life of your project, it's good to have some goals. What are your project's next steps for leadership and sustainability?

Leadership

How are we identifying and developing leaders? What's currently working? What's not? What will it look like to be developing leaders well?

1.
2.
3.

Financial Sustainability

Are we financially sustainable? How will we know what we need to be sustainable? What systems will we need to ensure sustainability? What's currently working? What's not? What will financially sustainability look like for us?

1.
2.
3.

Collaboration Covenant

How will your team *hub* and *extend*? Write a paragraph that captures the core messages of how your team will collaborate with others to multiply missional initiatives and churches in and beyond your city.

GOALS AND OBJECTIVES

What are your goals and objectives for the next year? Often the work that you've done in the above sections will give you some important clues. Please list six.

This is where the MAP gets most specific. We encourage you to use numbers and dates, so that things become measurable. We have included some examples. List your goals and in order of importance. Make your statements short and clear and limit them to what you hope to achieve in the next 12 months

Sample goals:

1. To have 3 vision meetings by July 15th, 2018, with about 20 people in attendance.

2. To organize 2 monthly social events for the rest of this year.

3. To start an Alpha course by April 31st with 10 people in attendance.

4. To recruit an additional team member who can help in the areas of music and worship.

Our Team's Goals

1.

2.

3.

4.

5.

6.

Thank you for hard work! May God establish the work of your hands (Ps 91)!

Appendix B

The "Ministry of *Peripateo*"

Another useful immersing and listening practice is what Communitas' Dr. Wesley White calls the *"ministry of peri-pateo."* *Peripateo* is a Greek word often used by the New Testament writers to describe one's movement through daily life routines, literally meaning "walking" *(pateo)* "around" *(peri-)*. We see a form of the word used, for example, in Col. 4:5 - "Use your heads as you *live and work among (peripateite) outsiders*" (NIV). In the early years of planting Mosaic Church in Glasgow, Scotland, Wes and his missionary team instituted the "ministry of walking about" as a regular rhythm for the leadership team. Members of their core team regularly set out, individually or two-by-two, to walk the streets and parks of their area for an hour or two. As they moved about on foot, each person sought to be prayerfully attentive to all sensory data coming in. They may engage an occasional neighbor in conversation, or they might drop into some local shops, businesses, or community centers, all the while praying and asking God to help them pay attention to important things they might not otherwise see.

While out walking one morning, Wes says his heart was feeling light but full, and he began to sing aloud. An older man drawn by the unusual public singing set out in Wes' direction and followed behind Wes with a curious look on his face. At a certain point Wes noted the man's presence, and he paused to engage him in conversation. When the man asked Wes why he was singing, Wes explained that it was overflow of joy from his heart as he was walking and praying for the city and for the people he encountered. The man was visibly moved to hear that Wes and his group would engage in such a caring activity for the sake of others. God had touched somebody in an unexpected way as space was made to walk about in Christ's name.

Another version of this ministry of walking around might involve a team researching their city and developing a spiritual map of a sort, to be used as a regular prayer pilgrimage for their group. Prayer walking, in whatever form, helps teams both to keep their discerning ears open and also add to their growing base of knowledge about their city.

Consider the following questions as you develop your own practice of *Peripateo*:

- *How frequently will our team practice prayer walking?*
- *Who will participate?*
- *How will we "cover" our neighborhood with prayer walking?*
- *What route(s) will we take?*
- *Where are the neighborhood hotspots, parks, cafes, and other places of interest where people gather?*
- *Who have we met on our prayer walks, and what do we sense God is saying in each of those encounters?*
- *What do we sense God is saying to us about our surroundings, and what historic markers help us understand this area from a spiritual perspective?*
- *What needs are we discovering in the neighborhood as the result of our prayer walks?*
- *What about the neighborhood are we celebrating as the result of our prayer walks (e.g. what assets or signs of shalom are evident)?*
- *Where are we recording and sharing the significant findings from our walking?*

Appendix C

Conducting a Neighborhood Exegesis Exercise

We're going to take time observing and learning a bit about a part of our city. As we walk and observe and listen in groups of 2-4 people, the questions below will help us see and experience our city in new ways. They will also help inform our understanding of and responsiveness to the neighborhoods and social groupings in this particular area. We will end by reflecting on what it might mean to seek the *shalom* of these places (Jeremiah 29:7).

1. As you stand at your starting point, what do you see as you look in each direction? What do you hear or sense? What activities do you notice?

As you begin to walk about...

2. What do you notice about the front yards or entries to each of the houses or apartments?
3. Does this neighborhood or part of the city feel like a cared-for place?
4. How many houses, apartment flats, or buildings for sale do you see? What signs of transience do you observe?
5. What do you notice about the parks? Are they inviting places? Who is there?
6. Do you notice churches or religious buildings? What does their appearance communicate?
7. What kinds of commercial buildings are there? Who occupies them?
8. Describe the people you see walking about or tending to their homes/yards or businesses.
9. In what ways are people, bicycle, and auto traffic flow managed? Where do you note sidewalks, lights, or crosswalks and pedestrians?
10. Are there places in this neighborhood that you would not go into? Why?
11. Where are the places of life, hope, beauty, or community in this neighborhood?
12. What evidence of struggle, despair, neglect, and alienation do you see?
13. In what ways do you see evidence of God's presence in this area?

Along the way, engage in these three important actions:

1. Find an approachable person to talk with. Ask them these open questions:
   - What is most important to you for your life?
   - What are the concerns of your neighbors and your neighborhood?
   - What needs immediate attention in your neighborhood?
   - What does your neighborhood do well or contribute to the city?

2. With your partner, find a local hangout and get something to eat or drink. What do you hear and notice in that place?

3. Find a relic or symbol of your experience in the community and bring it back with you. You will be asked to share how this represents what your group experienced in your listening adventure together.

Appendix D

Open and Closed Questions

Open and closed questions are easy to discern. A closed question can be answered with one word, commonly yes or no, or a short phrase, such as "it is seven o'clock," or "she is 6 months old." Closed questions supply facts while keeping the control of the conversation in the hands of the interviewer, rather than the one who answers the questions. A closed question is a gracious way to invite a person into a conversation because it is low risk, typically requires less intimacy or self-revelation. Closed questions are often used to acquire qualitative and quantitative research. Closed questions use words like: *do, would, are, will,* and *if.*

Examples of closed questions:
- *Are you satisfied that these actions will change things?*
- *Will you consider another way to look at this situation?*
- *Do you think the meeting accomplished our goals?*

However, if you are hoping for a deeper encounter with people, you will want to follow with open questions. Open questions are used for narrative research (learning about people through their stories), and that is what you need to do here. Open questions deliberatively invite storytelling and self-disclosure. In other words, they hope for longer answers, whereby the control of the conversation passes from the interviewer to the one being interviewed. Through open questions the interviewer is inviting the respondent to think and reflect, give opinions and feelings. Open questions typically begin with: *what, why, how,* and *describe.*

Examples of open questions:
- *How do you see these actions leading to the change you desire?*
- *What would this situation look like if you viewed it from the perspective of each of your teammates?*
- *What could you have done differently in that meeting to make it more of a win-win outcome for everyone?*

Adapted by Deborah Loyd from www.changingminds.org.

Dynamic Adventure

Appendix E

Creating Margins for Spontaneity

1. Clear your desk, put your phone away, and cover any clock that is within sight. Get a fresh sheet of paper and a pen or pencil. Write at the top of the paper: *My Relationship with Time*. Begin by praying for the Holy Spirit to speak to you via the metaphor of Time.

2. Take a few minutes in quiet contemplation reviewing your day so far. Then review the past week. Consider how you use your time, how tightly your appointments and duties are booked. Notice when you have time margins and when you don't. What are your biggest frustrations regarding time? Talk to "Time" and allow "Time" to talk back to you. Begin by writing "Time, we need to talk about our relationship."

3. Now write about your use of time responding to these questions:
   - *Talk to "time" as you would a person, describing your relationship.*
   - *Describe how you and "time" do with the issues of proximity, frequency, and spontaneity.*

4. Then respond to these prompts:
   - *Are you happy with your use of your time? Why or why not?*
   - *How tightly are you booked? How does time squeeze you? Describe this.*
   - *Does time leave you margins in your days and weeks? If not, where would you like to see them?*
   - *What kind of relationship with time would give you margins to do what you want to do?*
   - *What could you do or stop doing specifically to create greater time margins for contextual ministry?*

   Follow the conversation until it is exhausted.

5. Ask the Holy Spirit to help you create a plan that will help you be who you need to be. What can you do specifically to create margins for mission, for doing contextual ministry? How will you do this? Write a plan of action, commit to it, and tell your mentor what you have learned.

Appendix F

Lectio Divina

This method of prayer goes back to the early monastic tradition. There were not Bibles for everyone and not everyone knew how to read. So the monks gathered in chapel to hear a member of the community reading from the scripture. In this exercise they were taught and encouraged to listen with their hearts because it was the Word of God that they were hearing.

When a person wants to use *Lectio Divina* as a prayer form today, the method is very simple. When one is a beginner, it is better to choose a passage from one of the Gospels or epistles, usually ten or fifteen verses. Some people who regularly engage in this method of prayer choose the epistle or the Gospel for the Mass of the day as suggested by the Catholic Church.

First one goes to a quiet place and recalls that one is about to listen to the Word of God. Then one reads the scripture passage aloud to let oneself hear with his or her own ears the words. When one finishes reading, pause and recall if some word or phrase stood out or something touched one's heart. If so, pause and savor the insight, feeling, or understanding. Then go back and read the passage again because it will have a fuller meaning. Pause again and note what happened. If one wants to dialogue with God or Jesus in response to the word, one should follow the prompting of one's heart. This kind of reflective listening allows the Holy Spirit to deepen awareness of God's taking the initiative to speak with us.

Lectio Divina can also be an effective form for group prayer. After a passage is read, there can be some extended silence for each person to savor what he or she has heard, particularly noting whether any word or phrase became a special focus of attention. Sometimes groups invite members, if they so desire, to share out loud the word or phrase that struck them. This is done without discussion. Then a different person from the group would read the passage again with a pause for silence. Different emphases might be suggested after each reading: What gift does this passage lead me to ask from the Lord? What does this passage call me to do? The prayer can be concluded with an Our Father.

Whether one prays individually or in a group, *Lectio Divina* is a flexible and easy way to pray. One first listens, notes what is given, and responds in a way one is directed by the Holy Spirit.

Excerpt taken from "Praying with Scripture" by Douglas J. Leonhardt, S.J., selected from the chapter "Prayer and Decision Making in the Ignatian Tradition," in *Finding God in All Things: A Marquette Prayer Book* © 2009 Marquette University Press. Used with permission. All rights reserved.

Appendix G

The Ignatian Examen

This exercise is based on/adapted from Ignatius Loyola's *Spiritual Exercises*. This is probably most effective when written down, but these questions can also simply be prayed through.

- Ask God to help you identify the moment today for which you are most grateful. Recall that moment in as much detail as possible. What made it so special?

- Ask God to help you identify the moment today for which you are least grateful. What made it so difficult?

- Follow this with "When did I feel most alive today? When did I most feel life draining out of me today?"

Try to keep the Daily Examen as consistently as possible. At regular intervals look back over your journal entries and consider:

- What might these writings be telling you about how God is speaking to you?

- What do these writings suggest about your identity? Your purpose? Your direction?

Appendix H

Movements in Corporate Leadership Discernment

The following is a summary of Ruth Haley Barton's movements in corporate leadership discernment.

Get Ready:
Preparation

- Clarify the question for discernment.
- Gather the community for discernment.
- Affirm (or reaffirm) guiding values and principles.

Get Set:
Putting ourselves in a position to be led

- Prayer for indifference.
- Test for indifference.
- The prayer for wisdom.
- The prayer of quiet trust.

Go:
Discerning God's will together

- Set the agenda for listening.
- Listen to each other.
- Listen to God in silence.
- Reconvene and listen again.
- Identify and work with options.
- Agree together.
- Seek inner confirmation.
- Affirm God's guidance.

Do: The will of God

- Communicate with those who need to know.
- Make plans to do God's will as you have come to understand it.
- Keep discerning as you do God's will.

Appendix I

A Process for Determining a Community's Values

A *value* is that which matters most to us as a spiritual community; the ideal(s) we insist on expressing together.

Time: 2 to 3 hours in two sessions
Supplies: Paper, pens or pencils, sticky-notes, whiteboard and markers

NOTE: Make sure you capture what you intend to actually live out. Too many values statements end up with one or more values that remain latent or inactive. As a team, you're after *actual values*, not *aspirational values*. This is why a community must road-test or practice whatever they define as values to verify them as *actual* values.

Schedule several hours together as a leadership team to work on determining a "starter set" of values. These will have to be tested by life together and by the wider community, but you have to start somewhere.

1. Allow ten minutes for participants to write out their personal responses to the following questions:
    *   *What would you really like this community to stand for?*
    *   *What would a church community have to be about for you to really own it as home?*

2. Each person records three to five of these statements on sticky-notes, one per note (also include each person's name or initials on each sticky-note).

3. Each person shares his responses, placing his sticky-notes on the whiteboard as he shares it. As individuals share, the facilitator captures the content, keeping a running record of what each person views as important in community.

4. As a group, organize these into categories or themes. Then decide on one word or phrase to describe each category.

5. The facilitator records all the categories and statements, listing each category and showing the individual statements that support that category. Everyone receives a copy of this draft to reflect on in the next week.

6. The next time you come together as a team, distribute the draft of group values to each person. Review the values and supporting statements together and adjust them as necessary based on your reflection from the previous week. The group will finish with four to eight values and statements that define them.

Appendix J

Common Christian Beliefs

Below is a list of belief statements compiled from various Christian faith traditions. It is meant solely as a resource to promote discussion in the *Discerning Conflicts Over Core Beliefs* learning exercise in chapter 5. This list is not intended to be an exhaustive list of Christian belief, nor is intended as a statement of theology by Communitas International.

There is only one God.

God is three in one or a Trinity.

God is omniscient or "knows all things."

God is omnipotent or "all powerful."

God is omnipresent or "present everywhere."

God is sovereign.

God is holy.

God is just or "righteous."

God is love.

God is true.

God is spirit.

God is the creator of everything that exists.

God is infinite and eternal. He has always been God.

God is immutable. He does not change.

The Holy Spirit is God.

Jesus Christ is God.

Jesus became a man.

Jesus is fully God and fully man.

Jesus was sinless.

Jesus is the only way to God the Father.

Man was created by God in the image of God.

All people have sinned.

Death came into the world through Adam's sin.

Sin separates us from God.

Jesus died for the sins of each and every person in the world.

Jesus' death was a substitutionary sacrifice. He died and paid the price for our sins, so that we might live.

Jesus resurrected from the dead in physical form.

Salvation is a free gift of God.

The Bible is the "inspired" or "God-breathed," Word of God.

Those who reject Jesus Christ will go to hell forever after they die.

Those who accept Jesus Christ will live for eternity with him after they die.

Hell is a place of punishment.

Hell is eternal.

There will be a rapture of the church.

Jesus will return to the earth.

Christians will be raised from the dead when Jesus returns.

There will be a final judgment.

Satan will be thrown into the lake of fire.

God will create a new heaven and a new earth.

© 2016 About.com. Mary Fairchild, "Basic Christian Beliefs," http://christianity.about.com/od/christiandoctrines/a/basicdoctrines.htm. Used by permission.

Appendix K

The Church Beautiful
Dr. Wesley White

In my family we have developed a tradition that has proven to be not only essential, but also deeply cherished by each one of us. At birthdays, along with a special meal and cake and, of course, presents, we also go around the family circle offering words of love and affirmation to the birthday person. We tell them explicitly what it is about them that we so love and why we so appreciate them. We give them examples and describe their characteristics that so endear them to all of us. We celebrate their lives among us with words and prayers that reach down into the soul and bring blessing.

In a similar way, I want to celebrate the Church. It is, of course, more in vogue these days to defend a chasm we would rather maintain between the Jesus we admire and his Church for which we are, honestly, embarrassed. But I want to suggest that although this gulf is to some measure understandable, it is nonetheless both erroneous and unhealthy. It certainly goes against the grain of major portions of New Testament material. On the contrary, I think we can legitimately recite a litany of what attires the Church with beauty, what raises it up as laudable, what causes it to be appreciated in many quarters of the world. Without shoving serious weaknesses and problems under the proverbial carpet, I think we can, at the same time, openly and ardently confess all that we love about the Church.

I love the *simplicity* of the Church. I so appreciate the simple act of people coming together weekly to sing and pray and hear and apply the Word of God and share in the Eucharistic meal. It demonstrates the joy to be had in the sharing of lives so bracketed by a weekly routine and in small groups that gather at intermittent times. It rather simply provides for a myriad of ways in which encouragement for folk takes place.

I love the *consistency and faithfulness* of the Church. I recently met a fellow at a conference in Derbyshire, England, who attends an Anglican Church which has had uninterrupted ministry in that area since the year 811 c.e.—twelve hundred and two years of ongoing ministry in the name of Jesus. Consistency like this is so often matched by a real sense of *authenticity*, as local churches are not usually a collecting pool of the powerful and elite and wealthy, but people fraught with fragility and weakness and struggle and honesty and hope.

I love the *giving nature* of the Church. We should note that the United Nations' Report on Social Renewal, November 2011, tells us that 67% of the most effective philanthropy in the last fifty years can be attributed to local Christian congregations around the world. In its wake is a more than credible level of *transformational effectiveness*, such that urban studies today confirm that the Christian Church is responsible for, by far, the greater incentive for the development of hospitals and universities and cultural centers and services to the poor and to the advancement of civil and human rights in almost all the major cities of the world.

I love the *focus* of the Church on Jesus Christ, who alone can change people from the inside out and change the world from the outside in. It focuses, in fact, on *the message* of the Church, the good news that God so loved the world that in Jesus Christ, the very Son of God, he has begun the renewal of all things, God's re-creative purposes, and the end of all that is evil, all that is the result of the destructive designs of the evil one.

And I love the *people* of the church who are learning through all sorts of ups and downs, and through joys and struggles, what it is to be the people of God; how to trust this one and only God and serve him, and how to invite all and everyone into his inclusive embrace. I love the *missionary courage and zeal* of this Church, which has sent these same people into every corner of the globe, into some of the harshest and most dangerous sectors, giving up huge bits of personal preference in order to show and share the love of Christ.

And I could go on and on about all that I love about the Church.

So what does this verbal litany have to do with any sort of overture to Paul's letter to the Ephesians? As we shall see—everything! What themes does it portend? What motifs arise? They are, as we shall discover, many and varied, but with an overarching emphasis. There is, in other words, every reason to extol the Church in the world.

Clearly, the main goal of the Ephesian letter is the Apostle Paul's theology of Christ for the Gentiles. In other words, Christ for the world, in what is undoubtedly a missionary epistle. The heart of this affirmation is expressed in 3:4-8, "...when you read you can understand my insight into the mystery of Christ, which in other generations was not made known to the sons of men, as it has now been revealed to His holy apostles and prophets in the Spirit; to be specific, that the Gentiles are fellow heirs and fellow members of the body, and fellow partakers of the promise in Christ Jesus through the gospel——To me, the very least of all saints, this grace was given, to preach to the Gentiles the unfathomable riches of Christ..."

A detailed reading of Ephesians, however, might lead us to more precisely suggest the broader theme of Christ for the world *through the Church*. It is the Church, after all, that is the contextually consistent place for the missional preaching that Paul has in mind. As in 1:22-23, "And He put all things in subjection under His feet, and gave Him as head over all things to the church, which is His body, the fullness of Him who fills all in all."

On this account, Markus Barth contends that the overarching theme of the Ephesian Letter of Paul is nothing less than *the cosmic Christ at work in the world through the universal, but locally-based, Church of Jesus.* More specifically, Barth offers that "only in Ephesians is the very essence of the church directly identified with her stance before, her service to, and if need be her resistance against, all angels and demons, all periods and spirits that shape, represent, or terrorize the world."

Although the theological argument of Ephesians is complex, its structure is surprisingly simple. Harold Hoehner divides Ephesians into two easily discernible parts that he refers to as *the calling* of the church (chapters 1-3) and *the conduct* of the church (chapters 4-6). The "Amen" at the end of chapter 3 coupled with the commencing of clear and direct exhortation in the opening verses of chapter 4 mark these divisions out as deliberately and literarily composed.

As we examine the Apostle's deliberate structuring, of even greater import is the nature of what Paul inserts to separate the sections of the letter defined by doctrine and duty (the calling of the church and the conduct of the church). What we find is an incredibly potent and critically situated *prayer* in 3:14-21: "For this reason I bow my knees before the Father, from whom every family in heaven and on earth derives its name, that He would grant you, according to the riches of His glory, to be strengthened with power through His Spirit *in the inner man*, so that Christ may dwell in your hearts through faith; and that you, being rooted and grounded in love, might be enabled to comprehend, *with all the saints*, how wide and long and high and deep is the love of Christ, to know this love that surpasses knowledge—that you may be filled to the measure of all the fullness of God. Now to him who is able to do far more abundantly beyond all we ask or imagine, according to the power that is at work within us, to him be glory in the church and in Christ Jesus throughout all generations, for ever and ever! Amen." [emphasis mine]

Though there is so much worthy of delving into in terms of the theological content of the prayer, let's now note the structuring of this prayer around *two critical clauses*. Verse 16 provides the first of these with the prepositional phrase, "*in the inner man*" (εις τον εσω ανθρωπον), where it sets the parameters of what Paul is praying for—*personal soul development*, characterized by strength that is derived from the power of the Holy Spirit.

The second clause is found in Verse 18 and involves yet another prepositional phrase, "*with all the saints*" (συν πασιν τοις αγιος). This phrase sets the parameters of what Paul is praying for, in a contrasting way. Where the first phrase concerns the individual, this one pertains to what we might call the "collective comprehension" of Christ's expansive love. It deliberately specifies the collective experience ("with all the saints") as that context in which we might discover "how wide and long and high and deep is the love of Christ; to know this love that surpasses knowledge."

This entire Pauline prayer is constructed around those two divisions so that we can clearly see and hear what is so importantly suggested. Yes, this prayer confirms Paul's holistic concern for an inner enabling that is the result of the power of the Holy Spirit at work in the context of personal soul growth. But, if we hope to have any experience with, any capacity at all to comprehend this immense, expansive love of Christ—its width, length, height, and depth—it will only be as we do so *with all the saints*.

There are, as well, a number of critical factors to grapple with regarding what the Apostle means to suggest. First, when Paul uses the term, "to know," it is almost certainly the case that he is resorting to Septuagint vernacular that borrows from the Hebraic sense in which "to know" is an expression of sexual intimacy. It is imbedded in the Greek word γνωσκω (gnosko), but getting at that intimate experience of the love of Christ that is not limited to cognitive knowledge, but is more about intimate, experiential knowledge.

Second, when Paul uses this sort of dimensional language, by speaking of *width*, *length*, *height* and *depth*, it is very likely that he is lending his support to an emphasis in Wisdom literature, from both biblical and extra-biblical sources that has in view nothing less than the *four dimensions* of the entire cosmos. They may even refer to the four pillars of order which Jewish tradition listed as Law, Politics, Religion, and the Creative Arts.

This approach, therefore, to the collective comprehension of the expansive love of Jesus certainly includes our own overtly therapeutic experience as those who participate, empowered "in the inner man." But it is also much, much broader than that so as to embrace the width of the socio/religious structures of humanity as well as the length of the political realities that affect the whole world. It embraces the heights of creative-artistic freedoms that remind even the most depraved of a transcendent truth that beckons them, as well as the depth of the judicial equities or inequities that are meant to reflect the very heart of God.

These four dimensions are meant to implicate or involve (in the most positive of senses) the powerful love of Jesus Christ. This love is intended, via the Church, to impact the principalities and powers--to which the Apostle refers later in the epistle—that govern the orders and functions of the world. They are, in fact, those powers that attempt to dictate the very contours of the universe and, indeed, the entire cosmos. And they are only dealt with in a manner that is widely inclusive, referred to here by Paul as "with all the saints."

Finally, it is vital that we take aboard the ecclesiological significance of what the Apostle Paul has in mind with his inclusion of this seemingly insignificant little phrase, "with all the saints." It is not a simple statement of function or a simple reference to historical chronology. Rather, it is yet another metaphor for the localized Body of Christ. Andrew Lincoln states it best when he suggests that the caveat of the phrase demonstrates that the "comprehension the writer desires for his readers is not some esoteric knowledge on the part of individual initiates, not some isolated contemplation, but the shared insight from belonging to a community of believers."

It means, in other words, the Church and the Church's domain. We are to so grasp, so comprehend, the vastness of the love of Christ that we are able to envision its intended application to every single sphere of what it means to be human, in the broadest dimensions conceivable. That is to say that we, as a community, bring that love to bear upon the four dimensions that make up nothing short of God's cosmic agenda. And it is for this reason that this centrally situated prayer of Paul concludes with one of the most sublime benedictions in all of the Bible: "Now to Him who is able to do far more abundantly beyond all that we ask or imagine, according to the power that is at work within us, to Him be glory *in the church* and in Christ Jesus to all generations forever and ever. Amen" (3:21) [emphasis mine]

This church, so beautiful! How could we ever express enough accolades to capture all that she is and all that she is meant to be!

Appendix L

Study of Bible texts using *kletos*

"For many are invited [klētoi], but few are chosen." (Matt. 22:14)

Paul, a servant of Christ Jesus, called to be an apostle and set apart for the gospel of God... (Rom. 1:1)

And you also are among those Gentiles who are called to belong to Jesus Christ.
To all in Rome who are loved by God and called to be his holy people: Grace and peace to you from God our Father and from the Lord Jesus Christ. (Rom. 1:6-7)

And we know that in all things God works for the good of those who love him, who have been called according to his purpose. (Rom. 8:28)

Paul, called to be an apostle of Christ Jesus by the will of God, and our brother Sosthenes,
To the church of God in Corinth, to those sanctified in Christ Jesus and called to be his holy people, together with all those everywhere who call on the name of our Lord Jesus Christ—their Lord and ours... (1 Cor. 1:1-2)

...but to those whom God has called, both Jews and Greeks, Christ the power of God and the wisdom of God. (1 Cor. 1:24)

Jude, a servant of Jesus Christ and a brother of James,
To those who have been called, who are loved in God the Father and kept for Jesus Christ... (Jude 1:1)

"They will wage war against the Lamb, but the Lamb will triumph over them because he is Lord of lords and King of kings—and with him will be his called, chosen and faithful followers." (Rev. 17:14)

Appendix M

Vocational Preferences

Caregivers help the socially or financially challenged, or the disabled with their basic needs.

Connectors create venues where people can find common ground, to learn, share a meal or a common cause.

Creators curate the metaphoric and symbolic, and express meaning through atmosphere.

Communicators carry a message and will use any avenue so that the people on the other end receive it.

Problem solvers think and experiment their way through problems.

Helpers assist others in doing what they want or need to do through physical labor or giving of resources.

Adventurers relish the thrill of discovery, prefer to be the point person, and often love the outdoors.

Healers relieve suffering of all kinds and instinctively know how to make others feel better.

Organizers make sense out of chaos by ordering people and systems.

Activists notice inequities and seek to make them right. Often are heard to say, "Why isn't someone doing something about this?"[67]

---

67 Deborah Koehn Loyd, *Your Vocational Credo: Practical Steps to Discover Your Unique Purpose* (Downers Grove: Intervarsity Press, 2015).

Appendix N

Consequences of APEST Imbalance

Dysfunctions are likely to occur when one APEST gift becomes dominant over the other four. The single leader church is most at risk, but there are similar implications for leadership teams lacking APEST balance.

APEST If an apostolic leader dominates, the church or other organization will tend to be hard-driving, autocratic, with lots of pressure for change and development, and will leave lots of wounded people in its wake. It is not sustainable and will tend to dissolve with time.

A**P**EST If the prophetic leader dominates, the organization will be one-dimensional (always harking back to one or two issues), will likely be factious and sectarian, will have a "superspiritual" vibe, or, somewhat paradoxically, will tend to be either too activist to be sustainable or too quietist to be useful. This is not a viable form of organization.

AP**E**ST When an evangelistic leader dominates, the organization will have an obsession with numerical growth, will create dependence on effervescent charismatic leadership, and will tend to lack theological breadth and depth. This type of organization will not empower many people.

APE**S**T When pastoral leadership monopolizes, the church or other organization will tend to be risk averse, codependent and needy, and overly lacking in healthy dissent and therefore creativity. Such an organization will lack innovation and generativity and will not be able to be transfer its core message and tasks from one generation to the next.

APES**T** When teachers and theologians rule, the church will be ideological, controlling, moralistic, and somewhat uptight. A rationale, doctrine-obsessed, Christian gnosticism (the idea that we are saved by what we know) will tend to replace reliance on the Holy Spirit. These types of organizations will be exclusive based on ideology like that of the Pharisees.[68]

---

68 Alan Hirsch and Tim Catchim, *The Permanent Revolution* (San Francisco: Jossey-Bass, 2012), 48-49.

Appendix O

Leadership Books

The Leader's Journey: Accepting the Call to Personal and Congregational Transformation, by Jim Herrington, Robert Creech, and Trisha Taylor

In the Name of Jesus: Reflections on Christian Leadership, by Henri Nouwen

The Three Levels of Leadership: How to Develop Your Leadership Presence, Knowhow and Skill, by James Scouller

The Leadership Challenge 5th Edition, by James M. Kouzes and Barry Z. Posner

Making Room for Leadership, by MaryKate Morse

Crucibles of Leadership, by Robert Thomas

Shackleton's Way, by Margot Morrell and Stephanie Capparell

Spiritual Leadership in a Secular Age, by Edward Hammet

The Ascent of a Leader, by Bill Thrall, Bruce McNicol, Ken McElrath

Deep Change, by Robert Quinn

Overcoming the Dark Side of Leadership, by Gary MacIntosh and Samuel D. Rima, Sr.

Leadership from the Inside Out, by Kevin Cashman

A Failure of Nerve, by Edwin Friedman

Real Power: Stages of Personal Power in Organizations, by Janet Hagberg

Making All Things New: An Invitation to the Spiritual Life, by Henri Nouwen

Missional Spirituality: Embodying God's Love from the Inside Out, by Roger Helland and Leonard Hjalmarson

The Leadership Ellipse: Shaping How We Lead by Who We Are, by Bob Fryling

Eldership and the Mission of God: Equipping Teams for Faithful Church Leadership, by J.R. Briggs and Bob Hyatt

Deep Mentoring: Guiding Others on Their Leadership Journey, by Randy Reese and Robert Loane

The Gift of Being Yourself: The Sacred Call to Self Discovery, by David Benner

Appendix P

Hallmarks of Maturing Church

Without suggesting that our list is perfect or complete, nor without any attempt to rank the hallmarks by importance, Communitas' twelve hallmarks of maturing church are as follows:

1. **Activates People Into God's Mission by infusing and cultivating missional DNA**
    The faith community is teaching and modeling the Bible's central theme of God's heart for the world. The group maintains a consistent missionary posture among their context and ministry focus group(s). This involves exercising a posture of sustained listening and curiosity, while intentionally building key relationships (especially with non-Christians) and participating with the neighborhood and city in events, groups and shalom-sowing causes. The "missional gene" is continually being passed on through repeated cycles of modeling, training, and creatively inspiring the body in the theology and behaviors that promote the church's call to be "in but not of the world." (Gen. 12:1-3; Mic. 6:8; John 20:21-23; Matt. 24:14; 28:18ff; Luke 4:18; 10:1-12; John 1:1-18; Acts 1:8; I Pt. 2:9-10).

2. **Robustly proclaims the gospel and sees new followers of Christ emerge**
    The community proclaims the reign of God in both word and deed. It regularly evangelizes, practicing a set of loving, intentional activities aimed at initiating persons into Christian discipleship. Baptisms are common as a natural outcome of such proclamation. Leaders insure that the group or church is an inclusive and easily accessible community, where non-Christians can readily find spaces to belong and "try on" a Jesus lifestyle before they choose to believe and follow Christ. The church recognizes that God's "good news" is expressed in many layers within the grand Story of Scripture. And its members are continually equipped to share that story and bear witness to its central figure, Jesus Christ (Mark 16:15; Matt. 24:14; Rom. 10:13; I Thess. 2: 1-13).

3. **Pursues a growing awareness of its unique identity and calling**
    The core group, especially its leaders, are able to articulate a crisp, united sense of who they desire to be, where the group is going, and what God is calling them to do. Vision, mission, values, and church culture are clearly defined and articulated regularly. This often includes adopting a core metaphor or name that communicates meaning consistent with the desired identity and direction. The church often refers back to its core statements as a key part of setting good community boundaries, discerning what it ought to say "yes" to, and what it should avoid or not take on. (Eph. 1; 3: 2:20, 3:5; Heb. 11:1-12:2; I Cor. 11:2; Rev. 2).

4. **Roots itself in Scripture and in its connection with the historical and existing Church**
    Leaders have a united grasp on the core theology and doctrines on which the church is founded. The church vigorously interacts with and submits itself to the biblical narrative, while applying itself to learn from the wisdom, core affirmations, and varied traditions of the greater Body of Christ. (Deut. 6:4-9; Eph. 2:20; I Tim. 4:11-16; II Tim. 3:10-17: I Cor. 4:16-17; 7:17b; 11:1-2; 15:1-8; II Thess. 2:14-15; Heb. 4:12).

5. **Practices a clear, accessible pattern of discipleship that helps people grow in Christ**

The church has adopted a basic rhythm of communal habits, activities, and liturgy conducive to growing its people in their relationship with God, each other, and the world. They are collectively living into this rhythm, and showing people new to the church how to adopt this rhythm for themselves (II Tim 2:1-7). This "sacramental life" includes observing the Lord's Supper, Baptism, and other meaningful rites and rituals that tangibly display the deep and often hidden workings of God's grace. Leaders avoid projecting a false dualism between the sacred and the secular, demonstrating through the life and teachings of the church that all of life is deeply spiritual. (Matt. 5-7; Phil. 3:17; Eph. 4:21-25; Col. 3:5-17; I Tim. 4:7; 11-16; Heb. 10:24-25; 13:7-8).

6. **Prioritizes grace and biblical wisdom when handling conflict and growth issues**

Church leaders continually cultivate a culture of grace. They have a united stance on how the church addresses conflict between members, and this general process and guidelines are clearly articulated, taught, and made available to all members. Leaders also carry out loving, redemptive discipline when necessary (both to guard the community and foster positive change in the member(s) in question), and this also follows clearly articulated guidelines. (Matt. 18; Rom. 12:4-5; I Cor. 5:1-12; 12:14-16).

7. **Empowers a stable leadership structure that is healthy, diverse and sustainable**

The church governs itself by its own chosen elders or leaders, who both meet the biblical qualifications (e.g. I Tim. 3) and also represent a healthy diversity in gifts/perspectives (e.g. Eph. 4:11). The community, for its part, empowers its leaders and respects their role in cultivating the growth, interdependence, and protection of "the flock". The church has reached a sustainable leadership situation and is able to tend to its ongoing development (i.e. it is no longer dependent on the original planting team for its long range survival). (cf. also, I Thess. 5:12-13; Heb. 13:17; I Pet. 5:2).

8. **Offers pathways for people to join the church and own its identity and way of life**

Maturing churches grow by inviting participants to commit to and own the church as their own. This allows the community to be carried on the shoulders of many who agree to do their part to see it become all that God intends. The church for its part expresses its own commitment to support the growth of those joining, helping them to be appropriately involved in the church's life, development, and decision-making. By whatever process people are adopted into the church as participating members, the church avoids creating an exclusive culture of "the committed" versus the "non-committed." Instead, the body finds ways to include and value all people connected to the church, in the hope that they too may one day want to make a solemn, discerned commitment to the church community. (Rom. 12:5; 16:1-26; I Cor. 5:12-13; 7:17; I Pet. 5:2-4).

9. **Equips and coordinates members so that each serves in her or his giftedness**

The church moves increasingly as a coordinated, animated body, with all limbs and parts contributing to the whole. The church helps disciples understand and grow in their God-given design, find their place in the body of Christ, and participate in well-orchestrated movement toward the church's vision. It also remains discerning and sensitive to how God may be working in the lives of members, encouraging each to adopt ministry pathways that are most conducive to their growth as disciples. (Rom 12:3-8; I Cor. 12-14; Eph. 4:11-12; II Tim. 2:2; I Pet 4:10-11).

10. **Operates as a sustainable and generous, financially-stable community**

The church is able to meet its financial needs, so that it can rise to its vision and grow to its potential. It is appropriately transparent in its handling of money and wisely stewards the resources of its people, while also utilizing sound accounting and reporting conventions. The church conveys in a host of ways that it is a generous and hospitable community, and this is seen clearly in the lives of its leaders as well. (I Chron. 29; Gen 14:18-20; Deut. 26: 1-15; Matt. 23:23; Eph. 4:28).

11. **Embodies the gospel as a communal sign, foretaste and agent of God's Kingdom**

The church indwells the Christian story and intentionally acts as a communal sign, foretaste, and instrument of the Kingdom of God. By its actions and by the relational spheres it creates, it helps people to see and experience ways the Spirit is at work renewing all things. For, "It is the indwelling and embodiment of the Christian story that makes it comprehensible, and perhaps even appealing, to society. It is the actions of the Christian community that exegete the Christian message" (Stanley Hauerwas). (Luke 4:16-21; Eph. 1:13-14; 2:19-22; I Cor. 3:16; 15:20, 23; II Cor. 5:17-21; 6:16; I Tim. 3:15; II Thess. 2:13; Heb. 3:1-6; I Pet. 2:4-5).

12. **Multiplies disciples, leaders, missional initiatives, and churches**

Church leadership gives serious strategic attention to multiplication, looking not only to internal resources but also collaborating with other like-minded churches and organizations to cultivate local movements. A high value is placed on creating sustainable processes for training and developing servant leaders, missional pioneers, and church planters. At the same time life-on-life discipleship is encouraged within the local body, so that as many members as possible are pouring into the lives of others and also being challenged in their own development. The church also sees itself clearly in the light of its potential and real contribution to the global missional Body of Christ. (Matt. 9:37-38; 13:23; 33; 25:20; 28:18-20: I Cor. 3:6).[69]

---

69 This represents Dan Steigerwald's revision of the original Communitas list of hallmarks he composed in the book, *Grow Where You're Planted* (Portland: Christian Associates Press, 2013).

Index of Learning Exercises

Chapter 5 – Practice: Expressing Our Unique Identity

Chapter 6 – Mature: Growing Up as a Sustainable Faith Community

Chapter 7 – Hub and Extend: Multiplying Life Near and Far

Appendices

51181594R00117

Made in the USA
Middletown, DE
08 November 2017